Gooseberry Patch co.

5-Ingredient
family favorites

Oxmoor
HOUSE

5-Ingredient
family favorites

©2012 by Gooseberry Patch
2500 Farmers Dr., #110, Columbus, Ohio 43235
1-800-854-6673, **gooseberrypatch.com**
©2012 by Time Home Entertainment Inc.
135 West 50th Street, New York, NY 10020

Hardcover ISBN 13: 978-08487-3822-8
Hardcover ISBN 10: 0-8487-3822-5
Softcover ISBN-13: 978-0-8487-3452-7
Softcover ISBN-10: 0-8487-3452-1
Library of Congress Control Number: 2011924056
Printed in the United States of America
First Printing 2012

Oxmoor House
VP, Publishing Director: Jim Childs
Creative Director: Felicity Keane
Brand Manager: Vanessa Tiongson
Senior Editor: Rebecca Brennan
Managing Editor: Rebecca Benton

Gooseberry Patch 5-Ingredient Family Favorites
Project Editor: Emily Chappell
Senior Designer: Melissa Clark
Assistant Designer: Allison Sperando Potter
Director, Test Kitchen: Elizabeth Tyler Austin
Assistant Directors, Test Kitchen: Julie Christopher, Julie Gunter
Test Kitchen Professionals: Wendy Ball, R.D.; Allison E. Cox; Victoria E. Cox; Margaret Monroe Dickey; Alyson Moreland Haynes; Stefanie Maloney; Callie Nash; Catherine Crowell Steele; Leah Van Deren
Photography Director: Jim Bathie
Senior Photo Stylist: Kay E. Clarke
Associate Photo Stylist: Katherine Eckert Coyne
Senior Production Manager: Greg A. Amason

Time Home Entertainment Inc.
Publisher: Richard Fraiman
VP, Strategy & Business Development: Steven Sandonato
Executive Director, Marketing Services: Carol Pittard
Executive Director, Retail & Special Sales: Tom Mifsud
Executive Director, New Product Development: Peter Harper
Director, Bookazine Development & Marketing: Laura Adam
Publishing Director: Joy Butts
Finance Director: Glenn Buonocore
Assistant General Counsel: Helen Wan

Contributors
Editor: Adrienne Davis
Copy Editor: Stacey Loyless
Proofreaders: Rhonda Lee Lother, Barry Smith
Interns: Laura Hoxworth, Alison Loughman, Caitlin Watkze
Photographers: Lee Harrelson, Beau Gustafson, Mary Britton Senseney
Photo Stylist: Mindi Shapiro-Levine

To order additional publications, call 1-800-765-6400.
For more books to enrich your life, visit **oxmoorhouse.com**
To search, savor and share thousands of recipes, visit **myrecipes.com**

Cover: Quick & Easy Lasagna (page 202)
Page 1: Slow-Cooker Creamy Apricot Chicken (page 196)

Goose berry Patch®

5-Ingredient
family favorites

Chocolate-Marshmallow
Pie, page 269

Dear Friend,

Don't you love discovering a great-tasting recipe that doesn't require a pantry full of expensive ingredients? Often, the best dishes are made with just a few items. That's why we are so pleased to share this hand-picked compilation of *5-Ingredient Family Favorites* with you!

Now you can choose from more than 200 tasty recipes that are so simple and delicious. And every recipe has five main ingredients or less…with the exception of a few pantry staples like salt, pepper or oil. From this tried & true collection, you're sure to find a memorable recipe for every occasion.

For your next neighborhood get-together, choose quick starters like Sweet Onion Dip (page 25) or Cheery Cherry Punch (page 45). For breakfast, surprise your family with Farm-Style Cinnamon Rolls (page 67). And when you need a comfort food, try Old-Fashioned Potato Soup (page 93).

Take your pick from dozens of winning sides and salads like Pepper & Corn Salad (page 120) or Cheesy Ranch Potatoes (page 170). Five-ingredient main dishes such as Easy Chicken Dinner (page 232) will make suppertime delightful. And no one will skip dessert when you make delectable sweets as yummy as Cherry Dream Pie (page 262).

So turn the pages and take a look. You'll also find menus, clever kitchen tips and heartwarming stories from our recipe contributors. Whether you're cooking for family or friends, we hope this cookbook will make the job a little easier.

From our families to yours,

Vickie & JoAnn

contents

Reuben Appetizers, page 13

Grandma McKindley's Waffles, page 58

Garlicky Chicken & Redskin Potatoes, page 190

Open-Face Peach Pie, page 266

Feta Cheese Ball,
page 10

simple starters

Look no further for delicious starters made with just a handful of ingredients…this chapter is chock-full! On game days, grab a few items for Toss-It-Together Salsa (page 30). During the holidays, impress your guests with simple recipes like Holiday Stuffed Mushrooms (page 27). Or, in the morning, refresh yourself with an Orange Slushy (page 39). Turn the pages to find mouthwatering appetizers and beverages you can put together in a flash.

Feta Cheese Ball

(pictured on page 8)

This is not your typical cheese ball...the taste of feta gives it Mediterranean flair!

A great twist on an old favorite, I often double the recipe to give to family and friends.

Anne

8-oz. container crumbled feta cheese
8-oz. pkg. cream cheese, softened

2 T. butter, softened
1 T. fresh dill weed, chopped
1 clove garlic, minced
assorted crackers

Combine all ingredients except crackers. Beat with an electric mixer on low speed. When well blended, form cheese mixture into a ball and wrap in plastic wrap. Refrigerate at least 4 hours or overnight. Serve with assorted crackers. Serves 8 to 10.

Anne Richey
Syracuse, IN

place card perfection

For a simple, sweetly scented place setting, tie a few cinnamon sticks together with raffia, attach a mailing label as a name card, and lay a bundle across each plate.

Sausage & Parmesan Puffs

Bring along these puff pastries to a party, and they're sure to be a hit!

2 frozen puff pastry shells,
   thawed
1 egg

1 T. milk
6 T. grated Parmesan cheese
1 lb. ground pork sausage

Cut each pastry shell lengthwise into 3 strips. In a small mixing bowl, beat egg with milk. Brush the top of pastry strips with half of the egg mixture; sprinkle one tablespoon cheese over each strip. Divide sausage into 6 parts and shape each into a log the same length as the strips. Place one sausage log into the middle of each strip. Fold edges up to enclose sausage and pinch edges together. Brush tops of rolls with remaining egg mixture. Chill for 15 minutes. Place a sheet of parchment paper on a baking sheet. Cut each pastry roll into one-inch sections and place on top of paper. Bake at 400 degrees for 15 to 20 minutes or until sausage is cooked and pastry is lightly golden. Makes 20 appetizers.

Corrine Lane
Marysville, OH

custom kitchen creations

Create customized canisters with just a little craft glass paint. Add a flourish of script with the help of stencils, or add a simple initial in a color that matches the kitchen. Try etching cream on glass canisters for a touch of frost!

Reuben Appetizers

Put these mini Reubens together in minutes, and they'll be gone in seconds.

1 loaf sliced party rye
½ c. Thousand Island salad
   dressing

¾ lb. sliced corned beef
14-oz. can sauerkraut, drained
1½ c. shredded Swiss cheese

Spread bread with dressing; set aside. Slice corned beef to fit bread; place 2 slices on each bread slice. Top with 1 to 2 teaspoons sauerkraut; sprinkle with cheese. Arrange on an ungreased baking sheet; bake at 350 degrees for 10 minutes or until cheese melts. Serves 12.

Carol Hickman
Kingsport, TN

seasoning secrets

Combine two teaspoons garlic powder and a teaspoon each of dried basil, oregano and lemon juice for a no-salt seasoning for meats and vegetables.

Chicken-Salsa Dip

Scoop it out with tortilla chips or corn chips…perfect appetizer for a small gathering!

8-oz. jar salsa, divided
8-oz. pkg. cream cheese, softened
8-oz. pkg. shredded Mexican-
    blend cheese

2 to 3 boneless, skinless chicken
    breasts, cooked and diced
tortilla chips

Blend half the salsa with the cream cheese; spread on the bottom of an ungreased 9" pie pan. Top with remaining salsa; sprinkle with cheese and chicken. Bake at 350 degrees for 25 minutes. Serve with tortilla chips. Serves 8.

Margaret Collins
Clarendon Hills, IL

This recipe has been floating around our Bunco® group for a while. I'm not sure who originated it, but we all love it!

Margaret

spruce up your salsa

Almost any fresh veggie can be added to a favorite salsa recipe. Try stirring in chopped peppers, green onions, minced garlic and sweet corn.

Caesar Toast Appetizers

These crispy, savory bites are ready in no time at all.

1 egg, beaten
¼ c. Caesar salad dressing
8-oz. tube refrigerated crescent
    rolls, separated

2 c. herb-flavored stuffing mix,
    crushed
⅓ c. grated Parmesan cheese

Mix egg and salad dressing in a small bowl; set aside. Cut each crescent in half lengthwise, making 16 triangles. Dip triangles in egg mixture, then place in crushed stuffing to coat both sides. Place coated triangles one inch apart on an ungreased baking sheet. Sprinkle with Parmesan cheese. Bake at 375 degrees for 15 minutes. Makes 16 triangles.

Gladys Kielar
Perrysburg, OH

perfect timing

When whipping up a speedy supper, use a kitchen timer...let it watch the clock so you don't have to.

Cheese-Stuffed Peppers

Zesty peppers make a tasty appetizer for a party or potluck.

24-oz. jar whole mild banana
    peppers, drained
12-oz. container cream cheese,
    softened

6-oz. pkg. dried, sliced salami

Cut stems from peppers and remove seeds; rinse. Slice horizontally if needed to remove all seeds. Fill each pepper with cream cheese and wrap each with a slice of salami; secure with a dab of cream cheese or a toothpick. Makes 8 whole appetizers or slice each into thirds for approximately 2 dozen appetizers.

Jolie Newman
Yucca Valley, CA

Tuna Wrap-Ups

Create a best-loved appetizer with just a can of tuna and a few items from the fridge.

6-oz. can tuna, drained
2 T. mayonnaise
salt and pepper to taste

8-oz. tube refrigerated crescent
    rolls, separated
4 slices American cheese

Mix tuna, mayonnaise, salt and pepper; set aside. Arrange crescents on an ungreased baking sheet; set aside. Fold cheese slices diagonally and break into 2 pieces; place one piece on each crescent. Spread one heaping tablespoon tuna mixture over cheese; roll up crescent roll-style. Bake at 375 degrees for 12 minutes. Makes 8 rolls.

Sharon Hamill
Douglassville, PA

This is our family's variation on pigs in a blanket. The kids usually fight over the last one!

Sharon

Slow-Cooker Sweet & Sour Meatballs

Great as bite-size appetizers, you can also enjoy them as meatball sandwiches.

12-oz. jar chili sauce
16-oz. can cranberry sauce
2 T. brown sugar, packed
2-lb. pkg. frozen Italian meatballs

In a medium saucepan, combine chili sauce, cranberry sauce and brown sugar. Cook over medium heat until warm. Place meatballs in a 4-quart slow cooker; coat with sauce mixture. Cover and cook on high setting until heated through (about 2 hours), or on low setting for about 6 hours. Serves 10 to 15.

Becky Stewart
Alliance, OH

mistakes made right

Oops! If a simmering pot starts to burn on the bottom, don't worry. Spoon the unburned portion into another pan, being careful not to scrape up the scorched part on the bottom. The burned taste usually won't linger.

Crab & Broccoli Rolls

Season these rolls with onion or garlic salt to taste, or spice them up with a dash of hot pepper sauce!

6-oz. can flaked crabmeat, drained
10-oz. pkg. frozen chopped broccoli, cooked, drained and cooled

¼ c. mayonnaise
½ c. shredded Swiss cheese
8-oz. tube refrigerated crescent rolls, separated

Combine crabmeat, broccoli, mayonnaise and cheese; spread about 2 tablespoons on each crescent. Roll up crescent roll-style; arrange on a lightly greased baking sheet. Bake at 375 degrees for 18 to 20 minutes. Makes 8 rolls.

Jane Moore
Haverford, PA

herbed butter log

Make a tasty butter log using fresh herbs from the garden. Stir together butter, chives and shallots. Shape into a log and wrap in wax paper; refrigerate until firm. Roll in herbs and serve.

Spunky Spinach Dip

To add extra spice to this tasty dip, use medium to hot salsa.

Whether served with tortilla chips, fresh veggies or bread cubes, it's an irresistible dip.

Beverly

2 c. salsa
2 c. shredded Monterey Jack
   cheese
8-oz. pkg. cream cheese,
   softened and cubed

10-oz. pkg. frozen chopped
   spinach, thawed and drained
1 c. pitted olives, chopped

   Mix together all ingredients in a microwave-safe bowl; stir well. Microwave on medium setting until heated through. Serves 10.

Beverly Weppler
Atlantic, IA

keep it fresh

Store large bottles of olive oil in the refrigerator to keep them fresh. Pour a little into a small bottle to keep in the cupboard for everyday use.

Hot Parmesans

These toasty appetizers are sure to please at any potluck.

1 loaf sliced party rye
1 onion, minced
1 c. mayonnaise

¾ c. grated Parmesan cheese
⅛ t. Worcestershire sauce

Place bread slices on an ungreased baking sheet in a single layer. Mix together onion, mayonnaise, cheese and Worcestershire sauce; spread on bread. Broil 3 to 4 inches from heat source for 3 to 4 minutes or until toasted. Serves 15.

Fay Nielsen
Walkerton, IN

Kielbasa Sausage Bites

Serve the sausage warm with cheese and crackers.

2 lbs. Kielbasa sausage, sliced
1 T. oil
3 to 4 T. brown sugar, packed

1 T. vinegar
3 to 5 T. orange juice

In a large skillet, fry sausage slices in oil until brown; drain half of the drippings. Add brown sugar, vinegar and orange juice. Cook over low heat for 40 minutes, stirring occasionally. Makes approximately 7 to 8 dozen appetizers.

Elizabeth Cyr
Wallingford, CT

Sweet Onion Dip

The sweet spice of crunchy onion keeps guests coming back for more of this one-of-a-kind appetizer.

1⅓ c. shredded sharp Cheddar
    cheese
1 c. mayonnaise

1 c. sweet onion, grated
⅛ t. hot pepper sauce

   Mix ingredients together; spread in an ungreased 8"x8" baking pan. Bake at 350 degrees for 20 minutes. Makes about 3 cups.

Karen O'Brien
Midlothian, VA

No one ever believes this recipe is so easy. We love it served with corn chips.

Karen

no more tears

Place just a corner of a bread slice between your teeth while you're cutting onions, and your eyes won't water.

Holiday Stuffed Mushrooms

Start a memorable holiday tradition by making these mouthwatering mushroom tidbits.

8-oz. pkg. cream cheese, softened
1 T. dried, minced onion
2 t. Worcestershire sauce
1 lb. bacon, crisply cooked and
    crumbled
1½ lb. mushrooms, stems
    removed

Beat cream cheese, onion and Worcestershire sauce at medium-high speed until thoroughly combined. Stir in bacon; fill mushroom caps with mixture. Arrange on an ungreased baking sheet. Bake at 375 degrees for 15 minutes, or until tops of mushrooms are golden. Serves 6 to 8.

Jennifer Apthorpe
Panama, NY

I started making this recipe as a newlywed, and it became a signature appetizer. My husband's grandfather especially enjoyed them. Now when I make these mushrooms, I think of Grandpa Morton.

Jennifer

organize with style

Vintage carryalls are terrific for corralling clutter. Pick up a few to use in the kitchen, organize a craft room or display on a buffet table.

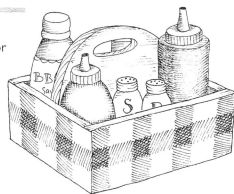

Sausage-Spinach Pitas

Hot and delicious...you may want to double this recipe!

1 lb. ground Italian sausage
10-oz. pkg. frozen, chopped
   spinach

2 c. shredded mozzarella cheese
⅛ t. nutmeg
12 small pita bread pockets

In a large skillet, thoroughly cook sausage. Add spinach, and cook until spinach is thawed; drain. Add cheese and nutmeg; toss. Spoon into pita pockets; place pockets on an ungreased baking sheet. Bake at 350 degrees for 20 minutes or until hot. Makes 12 pitas.

Grace Jackson
Honeoye, NY

keeping veggies fresh

A refrigerator's vegetable drawer is designed to keep fruits and veggies fresh and tasty. There are just a few exceptions...potatoes, sweet potatoes, onions and hard-shelled squash should be stored in a food-safe bin at room temperature.

Garden Vegetable Spread

Use this as a sandwich spread or as a delicious dip for your favorite sliced veggies.

8-oz. pkg. cream cheese, softened
½ c. cucumber, chopped
1 carrot, shredded
1 green onion, chopped
1 t. lemon juice
¼ t. dill weed

In a medium bowl, combine all ingredients. Chill before serving. Makes 1½ cups.

Michelle Campen
Peoria, IL

Ham & Olive Roll-Ups

Refrigerate the roll-ups for about six hours so the flavors can blend.

12-oz. pkg. boiled ham, chopped
2 8-oz. pkgs. cream cheese, softened
4-oz. can green chiles, drained and chopped
8-oz. can large, pitted black olives, drained and minced
8 10-inch tortillas

In a medium bowl, blend together ham, cream cheese, chiles and olives; spread mixture onto tortillas. Roll up tortillas jelly-roll style. Slice tortillas into one-inch pieces to serve. Makes 80 appetizers.

Melody Miller
Madison, WI

Toss-It-Together Salsa

Grab a few pantry staples and whip up this last-minute appetizer...don't forget tortilla chips!

2 14½-oz. cans petite-diced
   tomatoes
1 onion, diced

1 t. garlic, chopped
⅓ c. pickled jalapeños, minced
salt and pepper to taste

Combine all ingredients in a small bowl; stir well. Serve immediately or, if preferred, chill overnight. Serves 16.

Aaron Martelli
Santa Fe, TX

gifts from the kitchen

Family favorites like homemade salsa, jams and jellies are perfect hostess gifts...simply tie on a bow and gift tag!

Fruit & Nut Cheese Log

Cream cheese, fruit and nuts give this easy-to-make starter a unique zing of flavor.

8-oz. pkg. cream cheese, softened
1 T. apple jelly
¼ c. dried apricots, chopped

¼ c. dried tart cherries, chopped
¼ c. chopped walnuts
wheat crackers or fresh fruit

Place cream cheese on a sheet of plastic wrap; top with a second sheet of plastic wrap. Use a rolling pin to roll cheese to ½-inch thickness, approximately an 8"x6" rectangle. Remove top sheet of plastic wrap and discard. Spread jelly over cheese; sprinkle with dried fruits. Gently roll into a log, jelly-roll style. Roll log in chopped walnuts and wrap in plastic wrap; refrigerate until ready to serve. Serve with wheat crackers and fresh fruit. Serves 8 to 10.

Sharon Demers
Dolores, CO

This recipe is a frequently requested appetizer. It's very simple, yet so tasty!

Sharon

no-fuss chopping

Make chopped walnuts and pecans by placing whole nuts into a plastic bag and pounding with a meat mallet until desired size.

Reuben Bread-Bowl Dip

All the taste of the classic sandwich is in this cheesy dip.

2 16-oz. round loaves rye bread
8-oz. pkg. cream cheese, softened
1 c. shredded mozzarella cheese

2 2½-oz. pkgs. dried, chipped
    beef, diced

Hollow out the center of one loaf of bread; set aside. Cube removed rye bread and remaining loaf; set aside. Mix cheeses together; fold in chipped beef. Spoon into center of bread bowl; bake on a baking sheet at 350 degrees for 1¼ hours. Serve warm on a serving platter surrounded with bread cubes. Serves 8 to 10.

Mary Hastings
Gurnee, IL

bread-bowl supper

Hollow out a round loaf of pumpernickel bread to serve your chicken and noodles in...a quick and savory meal.

Fiesta Cheese Ball

This zesty cheese ball is scrumptious with tortilla chips or crisp bread.

I'm sure you'll be asked for this recipe and leave with an empty serving dish.

Amy

8-oz. pkg. cream cheese, softened
3 T. sour cream
2 T. taco seasoning mix
2 to 3 green onions, finely
    chopped

8-oz. pkg. shredded Mexican-
    blend cheese

Combine first 4 ingredients; form into a ball. Roll ball in shredded cheese. Wrap in plastic wrap and chill for at least 2 hours before serving. Serves 8 to 10.

Amy Hunt
Traphill, NC

terrific tablescapes

Festive trimmings can turn even a plain meal into a feast. Pick up some inexpensive, brightly colored napkins and table coverings at the nearest dollar store, and you're already halfway to a party.

Orange Slushy

Orange Slushy

Refresh yourself with a glass of soothing orange goodness.

6-oz. can frozen orange juice
    concentrate
¼ c. sugar

1 c. milk
1 t. vanilla extract
12 ice cubes

Place all ingredients in blender; blend to desired consistency. Serves 2.

Connie Pritt
Coalton, WV

I reward myself for mowing the lawn with this cool and nutritious creamy treat.

Connie

Minty Orange Iced Tea

A surprising, tasty twist on standard iced tea...try making this recipe with peppermint, spearmint or applemint.

6 c. water
8 teabags
¼ c. fresh mint, chopped
3 T. sugar

2 c. orange juice
juice of 2 lemons
ice

Bring water to a boil in a saucepan. Remove from heat and add teabags, mint and sugar; steep for 20 minutes. Discard teabags; strain out mint. Chill for at least 2 hours. Pour into a large pitcher; add juices. Serve in tall glasses over ice. Serves 6 to 8.

Barb Stout
Gooseberry Patch

Sometimes I find ginger mint or pineapple mint at the farmers' market and always pick up a bunch. It's fun to try a new herb in this iced tea recipe.

Barb

Frosty-Fizzy Punch

A scrumptious creamy combination of orange and vanilla...yum!

3 6-oz. cans frozen orange juice
   concentrate
2¼ c. water

3 T. vanilla extract
4 c. ginger ale, chilled
1 qt. vanilla ice cream

In a punch bowl, mix together orange juice concentrate, water, vanilla and ginger ale. Stir in ice cream to blend. Serves 10 to 12.

Jacqueline Kurtz
Reading, PA

Cinnamon Ice Cubes

Add a splash of spice to a tall glass of iced tea or soda.

These are a family favorite from Thanksgiving to New Year's Eve.
April

½ c. red cinnamon candies
½ c. water

3 c. orange juice

Combine candies and water in a medium saucepan over medium heat. Bring to a boil; simmer, stirring constantly, until candies are dissolved. Add orange juice; mix well. Pour into ice cube trays; freeze. Makes 4 to 5 dozen.

April Garner
Independence, KY

Berry-Citrus Smoothies

This super-tasty, three-ingredient recipe is ready in a snap.

1 pt. strawberries, hulled and
    sliced
1 c. buttermilk or plain yogurt

1 c. frozen lemon or orange
    sorbet

Combine all ingredients in a blender; process until smooth. Pour into glasses to serve. Serves 4.

Cheri Maxwell
Gulf Breeze, FL

main squeeze

Don't judge an orange by its skin. Pick the best by testing their firmness and how heavy they are for their size.

Tropical Smoothies

A chilled, fruity smoothie really hits the spot on a summer's day.

1 c. mango, peeled, pitted and
    cubed
¾ c. banana, sliced
⅔ c. milk

1 t. honey
¼ t. vanilla extract
Optional: 2 t. honey

Arrange mango in a single layer on a baking sheet; freeze for one hour. Place frozen mango and remaining ingredients in a blender. Process until smooth. Pour into glasses to serve. Serves 2.

Melissa Bordenkircher
Columbus, OH

spoonfuls of honey

Removing honey from measuring cups or spoons has never been easier…just coat your spoon or cup with vegetable oil before measuring the honey.

Cheery Cherry Punch

The sweet-tart flavors of cherry, apple, pineapple and lemon combine in this fruity concoction…along with a fizzy splash of ginger ale.

3-oz. pkg. cherry gelatin mix
1 c. hot water
46-oz. can pineapple juice, chilled
4 c. apple juice, chilled

¾ c. lemon juice
1 ltr. ginger ale, chilled
Garnishes: maraschino cherries,
    lemon wedges

Stir together gelatin mix and hot water in a small bowl until gelatin dissolves. Pour into a large pitcher, stir in juices; chill. When ready to serve, add ginger ale to pitcher, gently stirring to combine. Makes 3 quarts.

Beth Bundy
Long Prairie, MN

My grandma made this years ago…it was always a must-have at family gatherings.

Beth

fruity freshness

Add a burst of flavor to a glass of water…toss in fresh berries, melon or apple slices.

Sweetheart Shakes

Surprise your sweetheart with a frosty and refreshing shake!

3 c. milk, divided
1 c. vanilla ice cream, softened
3½-oz. pkg. instant vanilla
   pudding mix, divided

1 c. strawberry ice cream,
   softened
3 drops red food coloring

Pour 1½ cups milk into blender; add vanilla ice cream and ⅓ pkg. instant pudding mix. Cover; blend on high until smooth, about 15 seconds. Pour into 4 (8-ounce) freezer-safe glasses; freeze for 30 minutes. Pour remaining ingredients into blender; cover and blend until smooth, about 15 seconds. Pour into glasses on top of vanilla portion and serve. Serves 4.

Jessica Parker
Mulvane, KS

berry mix & match

Blueberries, raspberries, mulberries and strawberries are all scrumptious. For a flavorful change, mix and match berries in muffin, coffee cake and quick bread recipes.

Goldenrod Eggs,
page 50

breakfast & bread bonanza

This recipe collection proves you don't have to empty the pantry to make a fantastic breakfast. Wake up your family with Goldenrod Eggs (page 50) or Maple Ham & Egg Cups (page 60). And no need to fret about the perfect bread to go with your meal! These breads are sure to become favorites...Anytime Cheesy Biscuits (page 75) and No-Knead Jiffy Rolls (page 73).

Goldenrod Eggs

(pictured on page 48)

This simple dish will become a favorite comfort food as well as a great holiday breakfast.

5 to 6 eggs, hard-boiled, peeled and halved
6 T. butter or sausage drippings
6 T. all-purpose flour
2¾ c. to 3 c. milk
salt and pepper to taste
toast or split biscuits

Place egg yolks in a small bowl; mash and set aside. Chop whites and set aside. Place butter or drippings in a medium saucepan over medium-high heat; whisk in flour. Slowly pour in milk until desired consistency is achieved. Continue to heat through until mixture thickens. Stir in egg whites; season with salt and pepper as desired. Spoon over toast or biscuits. Sprinkle mashed egg yolks over each serving. Serves 4.

Fawn McKenzie
Wenatchee, WA

"egg-cellent" presentation

Search for vintage egg cups at tag sales and antiques shops…so pretty on the breakfast table or lined up on your kitchen windowsill! These dainty cups were made of everything from hobnail milk glass and porcelain to sterling silver.

Mexican Egg Bake

Refried beans make a perfect side for this dish.

12 corn tortillas, torn
16-oz. can green chili sauce
16-oz. pkg. shredded Cheddar
    cheese, divided

6 eggs
Garnish: sour cream; lettuce,
    shredded; and tomato,
    chopped

Layer tortillas, chili sauce and ¾ of cheese in an ungreased 13"x9" baking dish. Break eggs over top, spacing evenly. Sprinkle with remaining cheese. Bake, uncovered, at 350 degrees for 30 to 40 minutes. Slice into squares and garnish with sour cream, lettuce and tomato. Serves 8 to 10.

Nadine Watson
Aurora, CO

A south-of-the-border version of a quick breakfast casserole.

Nadine

time-saver!

Prepare your casserole the night before, cover, and refrigerate. Be sure to add 15 to 20 minutes to the cooking time.

Beef & Cheddar
Quiche

Beef & Cheddar Quiche

So yummy topped with sour cream or even salsa!

3 eggs, beaten
1 c. whipping cream
1 c. shredded Cheddar cheese
1 c. ground beef, browned
9-inch pie crust

Mix eggs, cream, cheese and beef together; spread into pie crust. Bake at 450 degrees for 15 minutes; lower oven temperature to 350 degrees and continue baking for 15 minutes. Serves 8.

Dianne Young
South Jordan, UT

No-Crust Spinach Quiche

Add chopped ham or crumbled bacon to this delicious crustless quiche for extra flavor.

10-oz. pkg. frozen chopped
    spinach, thawed and drained
Optional: ½ c. onion or
    mushrooms, chopped
6 eggs, beaten
½ c. milk
1 c. shredded Swiss or Cheddar
    cheese

Spread spinach in a greased 9" pie plate. Sprinkle onion and/or mushrooms on top, if desired. Beat together eggs and milk; stir in cheese. Pour egg mixture evenly over spinach. Bake at 350 degrees for 25 to 35 minutes, until top is golden and a knife tip inserted into center comes out clean. Cool slightly before cutting. Serves 6.

Mary Mayall
Dracut, MA

Your family will enjoy this easy dish any time of day.

Mary

Sausage Squares

These treats are just the right size to nibble on at your next brunch buffet.

2 c. shredded Cheddar cheese
½ lb. ground sausage, browned
2 eggs, beaten

1 c. biscuit baking mix
1 c. milk

    Place cheese in a greased 9"x9" baking dish. Sprinkle sausage over cheese. Combine eggs, baking mix and milk. Pour over sausage mixture. Bake, uncovered, at 350 degrees for 45 to 50 minutes or until golden. Cut into bite-size squares. Makes 8 to 10 squares.

Liz Sulak
Bryan, TX

flour power

Sift flour only when using cake flour. For general baking, just stir the all-purpose flour, spoon lightly into a measuring cup, and level off.

Apricot Oat Breakfast

Don't settle for ordinary oatmeal! Dried fruit, nuts and juice make these oats taste like dessert.

2 c. long-cooking oats, uncooked
⅓ c. slivered almonds
¾ c. dried apricots, chopped
¼ t. salt

1½ c. orange juice
1 c. water
¼ c. honey
Optional: milk

Combine oats, nuts, dried apricots and salt together in a large bowl; set aside. Whisk together orange juice, water and honey; add to oat mixture. Refrigerate, covered, for 8 hours or overnight. Serve cold, or if desired, topped with milk. Serves 4 to 6.

Stephanie Fackrell
Preston, ID

This delicious recipe is from my mom. She wanted us to eat a good breakfast and would tell us, "Breakfast-less children make unhealthy adults!"

Stephanie

Mom's Chocolate Gravy

A scrumptious way to jazz up leftover biscuits…the kids will ask for more!

1 c. sugar
1½ c. milk
1½ T. all-purpose flour

2 T. baking cocoa
2 T. butter

Combine all ingredients in a small saucepan over medium heat. Cook and stir until desired consistency is reached. Serves 8 to 10.

Teresa Ward
Halls, TN

My girls love this treat spooned over biscuits. When their friends sleep over, this is what they want for breakfast.

Teresa

Summertime Tomato Tart

Use your abundance of vine-ripe tomatoes in this summery treat.

4 tomatoes, sliced
9-inch pie crust
8-oz. pkg. shredded mozzarella
    cheese

2 T. fresh basil, chopped
¼ c. olive oil

   Arrange tomato slices in bottom of pie crust. Sprinkle evenly with cheese and basil; drizzle with oil. Bake at 400 degrees for 30 minutes. Let stand for 5 minutes before slicing. Serves 6.

Linda Belon
Wintersville, OH

tomato tip

No more trying to keep tomato plants upright in the garden. Plant pint-size cherry tomato plants in hanging baskets filled with potting soil. They'll grow beautifully... upside-down!

Sunday Skillet Hash

A traditional meat-and-potatoes morning meal you'll want to have again and again!

1 lb. ground pork sausage
2 lbs. potatoes, peeled and diced
1 onion, finely chopped
1 green pepper, finely chopped
salt and pepper to taste

Brown sausage in a large skillet; drain drippings. Stir in potatoes, onion and green pepper. Sprinkle with salt and pepper as desired. Cover and reduce heat to medium-low. Cook for 15 minutes or until potatoes are fork-tender. Serves 4.

Leianna Logan
Toledo, OH

This recipe conjures up some of my most favorite childhood memories. I have often doubled the hash, preparing it the night before and warming it in a slow cooker the next morning.

Leianna

sticky skillets no more

If your favorite non-stick skillet is sticky, fill it with one cup water, ½ cup vinegar and 2 tablespoons baking soda. Bring to a boil for a few minutes. Rinse well with hot water and wipe clean…no more stickiness!

Grandma McKindley's Waffles

You can't go wrong with an old-fashioned waffle breakfast...the topping choices are endless!

My great-grandmother lived to be almost 100 years old. She was a genuinely kind person as well as a great cook. She made her home such a nice place to visit.

Nicole

2 c. all-purpose flour
1 T. baking powder
¼ t. salt

2 eggs, separated
1½ c. milk
3 T. butter, melted

Sift together flour, baking powder and salt; set aside. With an electric mixer on high speed, beat egg whites until stiff; set aside. Stir egg yolks, milk and melted butter together; add to dry ingredients, stirring just until moistened. Fold in egg whites. Ladle batter by ½ cupfuls onto a lightly greased preheated waffle iron; bake according to manufacturer's directions. Makes 8 to 10 waffles.

Nicole Millard
Mendon, MI

sunny centerpiece

Fill a galvanized minnow bucket with bright and cheery sunflowers...a centerpiece that captures all the nostalgia of summertime.

Maple Ham & Eggs Cups

Ham and eggs make such a great breakfast or brunch...the kids will love the novelty too.

1 T. butter, melted	6 eggs
6 slices deli ham	salt and pepper to taste
1 T. maple syrup	English muffins, toast or
1 t. butter, cut into 6 pieces	biscuits

Brush muffin cups in pans with melted butter; line each cup with a slice of ham. Pour ½ teaspoon maple syrup over each ham slice; top with one pat of butter. Crack one egg into each ham cup; season with salt and pepper as desired. Bake at 400 degrees for 20 minutes or until eggs are set. Remove muffin cups from oven; use a spoon or gently twist each serving to loosen. Serve on English muffins, with toast or on split biscuits. Serves 6.

Staci Meyers
Montezuma, GA

quick-fix breakfast

Be creative with leftover dinner biscuits...spoon berries and whipped cream on them for a fresh dessert, or place a sausage patty and a cooked egg on one for a hearty breakfast.

Melon-Berry Bowls

Have a healthy start on sunny summer mornings with this fruity yogurt treat. Experiment with different kinds of melon and various yogurt flavors to find your favorite.

1 honeydew melon, halved and seeded
6-oz. container flavored yogurt

½ c. blueberries
1 c. granola cereal

Use a melon baller to scoop melon into balls. Combine melon with remaining ingredients. Spoon into individual bowls to serve. Serves 2 to 4.

Jill Ball
Highland, UT

pretty pedestals

Don't save pretty cake pedestals for just pastries...pile on fragrant lemons, limes and green apples for a splash of color.

Suzanne's Tomato Melt

Start your day with fresh garden flavor...hearty and delicious!

¼ c. shredded Cheddar cheese
1 onion bagel or English muffin,
   split

2 tomato slices
1 T. shredded Parmesan cheese

Sprinkle half the Cheddar cheese over each bagel or English muffin half. Top with a tomato slice. Sprinkle half the Parmesan cheese over each tomato. Broil about 6 inches from heat for 4 to 5 minutes or until cheese is bubbly. Serves one.

Audrey Lett
Newark, DE

I love this as a quick breakfast or snack, and it's so simple to make.

Audrey

extra eggs

If you find yourself with extra eggs on hand, it's easy to freeze them for use later in recipes that will be thoroughly cooked or baked. Whisk eggs well, and pour into a freezer-safe container. Be sure to label each container with the number of eggs inside, then freeze. To thaw, place the container in the refrigerator overnight, and use immediately.

Festive Brunch Frittata

An easy, gourmet meal that will impress your guests...also try it with mushrooms and spinach.

8 eggs, beaten
½ t. salt
⅛ t. pepper
½ c. shredded Cheddar cheese

2 T. butter
2 c. red, green and yellow
   peppers, chopped
¼ c. onion, chopped

Beat together eggs, salt and pepper. Fold in Cheddar cheese and set aside. Melt butter over medium heat in a 10" non-stick, oven-safe skillet. Add peppers and onion to skillet; sauté until tender. Pour eggs over peppers and onion; don't stir. Cover and cook over medium-low heat for about 9 minutes. Eggs are set when frittata is lightly golden on the underside. Turn oven on broil. Move skillet from stovetop to oven; broil top about 5 inches from heat until lightly golden. Serves 6.

Renae Scheiderer
Beallsville, OH

This is a special recipe I like to make on Christmas morning.

Renae

Farm-Style Cinnamon Rolls

There's nothing like waking up to the aroma of baking cinnamon rolls.

16-oz. pkg. frozen bread dough, thawed
¼ c. butter, melted and divided
¼ c. sugar
¼ c. brown sugar, packed
1 t. cinnamon

Place dough in a well-oiled bowl, and let rise to almost double its size. Roll out dough on a floured surface to a 14"x10" rectangle. Brush with 2 tablespoons butter; sprinkle with sugars and cinnamon. Starting on one long side, roll up jelly-roll style. Pinch seam together. Cut rolled dough into 12 slices. Coat the inside of a 9"x9" baking pan with one tablespoon butter. Arrange rolls in baking pan; brush with remaining butter. Cover and let rise in a warm place for 45 minutes to one hour. Uncover and bake at 375 degrees for 20 to 25 minutes, until lightly golden. Makes one dozen.

Cindy Adams
Winona Lake, IN

grandma's stain remover

Grandma knew how to remove stains from a favorite tablecloth. Combine half a teaspoon of salt with a tablespoon of water. Wet the stain, and lay the tablecloth in the sun. After an hour, gently rinse the tablecloth with cold water.

Lemony Poppy Seed Bread

Mini loaves wrapped in pretty plastic wrap make welcome gifts any time of year!

18¼-oz. pkg. lemon cake mix
3½-oz. pkg. instant lemon
    pudding mix

4 eggs
½ c. oil
1 to 2 t. poppy seed

Blend ingredients together; add one cup water, mixing well. Pour into 2 (8"x4") greased and floured loaf pans; bake at 350 degrees for 50 to 60 minutes. Serves 16.

Vicki Moats
Wyoming, IL

Fresh Raspberry Butter

You can substitute blueberries, strawberries, cherries or pineapple.

This butter is scrumptious on toast, waffles or pancakes.

Jacinta

8-oz. pkg. cream cheese, softened
½ c. butter, softened
1 c. powdered sugar

1 t. vanilla or almond extract
1 c. fresh raspberries, mashed

Combine all ingredients except berries; blend well. Gently fold in raspberries. Cover and refrigerate several hours or overnight. Keep refrigerated for up to one week. Makes 2 cups.

Jacinta O'Connell
Kenosha, WI

Italian Zeppoli Bread

This bread is an Italian Christmas Eve tradition.

1 pkg. active dry yeast
1 c. warm water, divided
1½ c. all-purpose flour

oil for deep frying
Garnish: powdered sugar

Heat ½ cup water until very warm, about 110 to 115 degrees. Dissolve yeast in warm water; set aside for 10 minutes. Stir flour and remaining water into yeast mixture; beat until a soft dough forms. Turn dough onto a lightly floured surface; knead until smooth. Place dough in a well-oiled bowl; turn dough to coat. Cover dough with a tea towel. Set in a warm place; let dough double in bulk, about one to 1½ hours. Fry 2-inch rounds of dough in 375-degree oil until golden. Drain on paper towels. Sprinkle with powdered sugar. Makes about 15.

fresh-baked gifts

Looking for a clever way to give a fresh-baked gift? Fill an old-fashioned sugar canister with Italian Zeppoli Bread…give with a shaker full of cinnamon and sugar.

Pecan Bites

These sweet bites don't even need frosting.

1 c. brown sugar, packed
½ c. all-purpose flour
1 c. chopped pecans

⅔ c. butter, melted
2 eggs, beaten

Combine sugar, flour and pecans; set aside. Blend together butter and eggs; mix into flour mixture. Fill greased and floured mini muffin cups ⅔ full; bake at 350 degrees for 22 to 25 minutes. Cool on a wire rack. Makes about 1½ dozen.

Hope Davenport
Portland, TX

autumn decor

Fill a shiny colander with plump red apples and mini pumpkins for an easy harvest centerpiece. Tie on a gingham ribbon, and tuck in a few sprigs of bittersweet as a finishing touch.

Homestyle Spoon Bread

Serve these golden rounds with butter, homemade jam or honey...delicious!

My mother grew up with this bread during the Depression. It looks like an English muffin but the inside is very soft...wonderful with butter and a cup of tea!

Tonia

1 c. all-purpose flour
2 t. baking powder
1 t. sugar

½ t. salt
oil for deep frying

Mix together all ingredients except oil; blend in ¾ cup water. Drop dough by tablespoonfuls into a heavy skillet filled with ¼-inch hot oil. Flip dough over when bubbles form along the edges; cook until golden on each side. Serves 4.

Tonia Holm
Burlington, ND

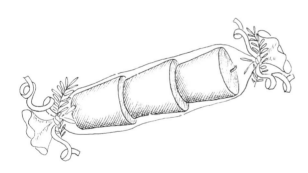

party favor in a flash

Lay votives end-to-end, and roll up in tulle. Tie the ends with curly ribbon for a quick gift or party favor.

No-Knead Jiffy Rolls

This is a beer bread turned into rolls...so delicious and simple to make.

3 c. self-rising flour
3 T. sugar
¼ t. salt

12-oz. can beer or non-alcoholic
beer, room temperature

Mix flour, sugar and salt together; add beer and stir well. Spray a muffin pan with non-stick vegetable spray; fill cups ⅔ full with dough. Bake at 375 degrees for 30 minutes or until rolls are golden. Serve warm. Makes one dozen.

Cheryl Hagy
Quarryville, PA

flour fix

Self-rising flour is handy for quick biscuits. If you're out of it, though, here's an easy substitution. For each cup needed, add 1½ teaspoons baking powder and ½ teaspoon salt to a measuring cup, then fill the cup level with all-purpose flour. Mix well before using.

Anytime Cheesy Biscuits

So easy...you can whip them up in minutes!

2 c. biscuit baking mix
½ c. shredded Cheddar cheese
⅔ c. milk

¼ c. butter, melted
¼ t. garlic powder

Mix together first 3 ingredients until a soft dough forms; beat vigoursly for 30 seconds. Drop by rounded tablespoonfuls onto an ungreased baking sheet. Bake at 450 degrees for 8 to 10 minutes or until golden. Whisk together butter and garlic powder; spread over warm biscuits. Makes about 1½ dozen.

Naomi Cooper
Delaware, OH

a brush of honey

To give your warm from the oven bread a sweet, shiny glaze, brush with honey...it also absorbs moisture, and your bread will stay fresh longer.

Savory Muffins

Add rosemary, thyme or basil to the batter for an aromatic version.

Even my husband can make these hearty muffins.

Carla

1 c. self-rising flour
1 t. baking powder

½ c. milk
2 T. mayonnaise

    Combine all ingredients; fill greased or paper-lined muffin cups ⅔ full of batter. Bake at 450 degrees for 20 minutes or until muffin tops are golden. Makes 6 muffins.

Carla McRorie
Kannapolis, NC

flea market finds

Keep an eye out for vintage cake stands at flea markets and auctions. Not just for cakes and pastries anymore, try them out as centerpieces for holding candles or fresh, colorful fruit.

Amish White Bread

This recipe makes two loaves...one for your family and one to share with the neighbors!

2 c. water	1½ t. salt
⅔ c. sugar	¼ c. oil
1½ T. active dry yeast	6 c. bread flour

Heat water until very warm, about 110 to 115 degrees. Pour water into a large bowl; add sugar and stir until dissolved. Stir in yeast until foamy; let stand for about 5 minutes. Mix in salt and oil; stir in flour, one cup at a time. Turn out dough onto a lightly floured surface, and knead until smooth. Place dough in a well-oiled bowl; turn dough to coat. Cover dough with a dampened tea towel. Set in a warm place; let dough double in bulk, about one hour. Punch dough down; knead for several minutes. Divide dough in half, and form into 2 loaves. Place in 2 well-oiled 9"x5" loaf pans. Cover again. Allow to rise for 30 minutes, or until dough has risen one inch above pans. Bake at 350 degrees for 30 minutes, until lightly golden. Makes 2 loaves.

Stacie Avner
Delaware, OH

This bread is awesome! The instructions might look long, but they aren't complicated if you follow them step-by-step.

Stacie

versatile centerpieces

A wooden dough bowl is so useful! When it isn't filled with rising bread dough, set it on the kitchen table and add shiny red apples for a quick and easy centerpiece.

Sour Cream Mini Biscuits

This recipe make several dozen bite-size biscuits...ideal for filling gift baskets or taking to a potluck.

Once you start snacking on these, it's hard to stop!

Jeanne

1 c. butter, softened
1 c. sour cream

2 c. self-rising flour

Blend butter and sour cream together until fluffy; gradually mix in flour. Drop teaspoonfuls of dough into greased mini muffin cups; bake at 450 degrees for 10 to 12 minutes. Makes 4 dozen.

Jeanne Barringer
Edgewater, FL

herbed biscuits

Add freshly-snipped herbs like dill weed, basil or thyme to biscuit dough for delicious variety.

Cheesy Onion Muffins

Use 12 to 15 mini English muffins for a bite-size variation.

3½ c. shredded Cheddar cheese
¼ c. onion, minced
¼ c. mayonnaise-type salad
   dressing

6 to 8 English muffins, split

    Mix cheese, onion and salad dressing together; spread over muffin halves. Arrange on a broiler pan; broil until golden. Slice muffins in half to serve. Serves 12 to 16.

Melinda Einan
Wrightstown, WI

a quick gift!

Give a jar of your homemade preserves with fresh-baked muffins from your favorite bakery wrapped in a pretty linen towel.

Focaccia Rounds

Try using a variety of seasonal, fresh herbs in this tasty creation...the possibilities are endless!

11-oz. tube refrigerated bread
    sticks
2 t. olive oil

1 t. Italian seasoning
2 T. fresh basil, chopped
2 T. grated Parmesan cheese

The perfect pairing with any salad.

Jackie

Remove bread stick dough from tube; do not unroll. Cut dough into 8 slices. Roll out each slice to a 4½-inch circle. Place circles on a greased baking sheet. Brush dough with oil; sprinkle with seasoning, basil and Parmesan cheese. Bake at 375 degrees for 10 to 15 minutes or until golden. Serves 8.

Jackie Smulski
Lyons, IL

keep your herbs fresh

Until they're ready for your best recipe, tuck sprigs of fresh herbs into water-filled Mason jars or votive holders for a few days. Not only will they stay fresh longer, they'll look lovely.

Parmesan-Garlic Biscuits

These upside-down biscuits are a hit with any Italian dish!

3 T. butter, melted
¼ t. celery seed
2 cloves garlic, minced

12-oz. tube refrigerated biscuits
2 T. grated Parmesan cheese

Coat bottom of a 9-inch pie pan with butter; add celery seed and garlic. Slice each biscuit into quarters; arrange on top of butter mixture. Sprinkle with Parmesan cheese; bake at 425 degrees for 12 to 15 minutes. Invert onto a serving plate to serve. Serves 8.

Jo Ann
Gooseberry Patch

quick kitchen decor

Add garlic braids to kitchen decor...hang them next to the door or alongside copper pots on a wrought-iron rack.

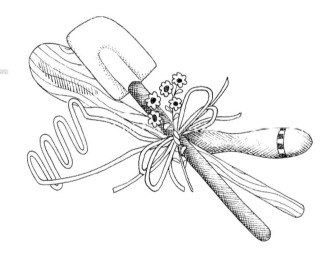

White Bean Chicken
Chili, page 86

sensible soups & stews

Here's an entire chapter of simple soup and stew recipes...you can count the ingredients on one hand! The kids will love the Cheesy Chicken & Noodle Soup (page 91). Need a speedy supper? Try Quick & Easy Chili (page 98). And the Chilled Melon Soup (page 111) is a cool choice for summer.

White Bean Chicken Chili

(pictured on page 84)

Add crusty rolls and a fresh salad for a hearty meal.

3 15.8-oz. cans Great Northern
    beans
4 boneless, skinless chicken
    breasts, cooked and cubed
16-oz. jar salsa

8-oz. pkg. shredded Monterey
    Jack cheese
8-oz. pkg. jalapeño cheese,
    shredded

    Add ingredients to a stockpot; heat over low heat until cheeses melt. Stir in up to one cup water for desired consistency; heat until warmed through. Serves 4 to 6.

Kristie Matry
Ada, MI

next-day soup

Here's a super-simple tip for scrumptious soup…and it doesn't cost a thing! Make soup ahead of time, and refrigerate for one to two days to let the flavors blend; then reheat and serve.

Garlicky Tomato Soup

This soup is especially tasty served with homemade bread brushed with melted herb butter.

3 tomatoes, cubed
2 green, red or yellow peppers,
    cut into bite-size pieces
10 cloves garlic, coarsely chopped
    and divided

½ c. olive oil
2 c. water
2 t. salt
pepper to taste

Combine tomatoes, peppers and half the garlic in a food processor. Pulse until tomatoes and peppers are chopped; set aside. Heat oil in a saucepan over medium heat. Add tomato mixture and cook, stirring often, about 5 minutes. Add remaining ingredients; bring to a boil. Reduce heat to low, and simmer for 10 minutes. Serves 4.

Diana Chaney
Olathe, KS

Summertime tomatoes are my absolute favorite vegetable... nothing even compares to them!
Diana

bottoms up!

Add cubes of toasted sourdough or herb bread to the bottoms of soup bowls, then ladle in your steaming soup. Yummy!

Slow-Cooker Beefy Taco Soup

Top each bowl of this hearty soup with sour cream and a sprinkling of shredded cheese.

1 lb. ground beef, browned
15-oz. can stewed tomatoes
15-oz. can kidney beans, drained
    and rinsed

1¼-oz. env. taco seasoning mix
8-oz. can tomato sauce

Stir together all ingredients; pour into a 3- to 4-quart slow cooker. Cover and heat on low setting for 6 to 8 hours; stir occasionally. Serves 4 to 6.

Erin McRae
Beaverton, OR

creamy & delicious

Give any chunky veggie soup a creamier texture...no cream required! Ladle out a cup of the cooked vegetables, and puree in a blender; then stir back into the soup and heat through.

Cheesy Chicken & Noodle Soup

Spice up this classic by topping it with shredded Pepper Jack cheese.

2 to 3 c. chicken, cooked and
    shredded
10¾-oz. can Cheddar cheese
    soup
4 to 6 c. chicken broth

8-oz. pkg. fine egg noodles,
    uncooked
1 c. milk
Optional: shredded Cheddar
    cheese

Combine all ingredients except milk and cheese in a large stockpot; bring to a boil over medium heat. Reduce heat; simmer until noodles are soft. Stir in milk. Spoon into bowls; sprinkle with cheese, if desired. Serves 6 to 8.

Christi Perry
Denton, TX

odor ouster

To keep your hands smelling sweet while cutting odorous onions, try rubbing your hands with the cut end of a stalk of celery.

Tomato & Spinach Soup

For a bisque-style soup, drizzle in some cream after removing the saucepan from the heat.

2 cloves garlic, minced
2 T. olive oil
14½-oz. can stewed tomatoes

14½-oz. can diced tomatoes
1 to 2 c. baby spinach

In a saucepan over medium heat, sauté garlic in hot oil until tender. Stir in both undrained cans of tomatoes. Cook on medium-low heat until warmed through. Add spinach; cook and stir until spinach is slightly wilted. Serves 4 to 6.

Joely Flegler
Tulsa, OK

sugary solution

To mellow the flavor of tomato soup, stir in a teaspoon of sugar.

Old-Fashioned Potato Soup

If you don't have time to peel and dice the potatoes, try using frozen diced potatoes for this soup.

8 potatoes, peeled and cubed	1 T. butter
4¼ c. milk, divided	½ c. all-purpose flour
salt and pepper to taste	1 egg, beaten

In a large stockpot, combine potatoes and 4 cups milk; season with salt and pepper. Heat mixture over medium-high heat for 15 to 20 minutes or until potatoes are tender. In a medium bowl, blend together butter and flour; add egg and remaining milk. Drop by teaspoonfuls into potato mixture. Cover and cook an additional 10 minutes, stirring occasionally. Serves 4.

Donna Zink
Lapeer, MI

There is nothing better than potato soup on a cold, blustery day...and this recipe's so easy!
Donna

Creamy Crab Stew

Serve with cheese crackers or crusty sourdough bread.

1 lb. crabmeat, cooked	10¾-oz. can cream of chicken
10¾-oz. can cream of celery	soup
soup	

Mix all ingredients together; fill empty soup can with water, add to soup. Mix well, and heat thoroughly without boiling. Serves 4 to 6.

Helen VonWaldner
Savannah, GA

Too-Simple Tortilla Soup

Top this soup with a couple of slices of avocado, fresh cilantro or a dollop of sour cream.

2 10-oz. cans chicken, drained
2 14½ oz. cans chicken broth
2 15-oz. cans white hominy, drained

16-oz. jar salsa
1 T. cumin

Combine all ingredients in a stockpot; bring to a boil. Reduce heat, and warm through. Serves 6 to 8.

Paulette Cunningham
Lompoc, CA

thick & nutritious

Save the water that potatoes are boiled in…add it to soups and sauces to add thickness, nutrition and flavor.

Slow-Cooker Country Chicken & Dumplings

Using refrigerated biscuits for the dumplings and a slow cooker to heat makes this recipe a lifesaver on busy weeknights.

> This is absolutely delicious down-home goodness with very little effort!
>
> Joanne

4 boneless, skinless chicken
   breasts
2 10¾-oz. cans cream of
   chicken soup

2 T. butter, sliced
1 onion, finely diced
2 7½-oz. tubes refrigerated
   biscuits, torn

Place chicken, soup, butter and onion in a 4-quart slow cooker; add enough water to cover chicken. Cover and cook on high setting for 4 hours. Add biscuits to slow cooker; gently push biscuits into cooking liquid. Cover and continue cooking for about 1½ hours, until biscuits are done in the center. Serves 6.

Joanne Curran
Arlington, MA

save with slow cookers

Slow cookers use very little electricity…no more than a light bulb, costing about two cents an hour. They're actually more economical than your oven.

Quick & Easy Chili

Simple and tasty…this chili is sure to become a mealtime classic.

This recipe was given to me many years ago by a close friend. Since then, it's become a dinnertime staple at our house. And it's just as yummy, if not better, the next day!

Carol

2 lbs. ground beef
2 T. oil
2 15-oz. cans kidney beans,
    drained and rinsed

2 10¾-oz. cans tomato soup
2 T. chili powder

Brown ground beef in hot oil; drain. Add remaining ingredients plus one empty soup can filled with water; stir well. Bring to a boil; reduce heat, cover and simmer for one hour. Serves 6 to 8.

Carol Shirkey
Canton, OH

skillet rescue

To easily remove burned or stuck-on food from your skillet, simply add a few drops of dish soap and water to cover the bottom of the pan, and bring to a boil.

Easy Cabbage Stew

In a hurry? Pick up a bag of coleslaw mix, and there's no need to shred any cabbage.

1 head cabbage, shredded
1 lb. smoked sausage, sliced

10¾-oz. can cream of celery soup
salt and pepper to taste

Place cabbage and sausage in a large soup pot; add just enough water to cover. Simmer over medium heat for about 20 minutes, until cabbage is tender. Do not drain. Stir in soup, salt and pepper; heat through. Serves 4 to 6.

Teresa Stiegelmeyer
Indianapolis, IN

cider pizzazz

A dash of cider adds zing to any cabbage dish.

Slow-Cooker Butternut Squash Soup

2½ lbs. butternut squash,
    halved, seeded, peeled and
    cubed
2 c. leeks, chopped
2 Granny Smith apples, peeled,
    cored and diced

2 14½-oz. cans chicken broth
1 c. water
seasoned salt and white pepper
    to taste
Garnish: freshly ground nutmeg
    and sour cream

Just chop a few ingredients and combine in the slow cooker for a delicious gourmet soup...so easy!

Combine squash, leeks, apples, broth and water in a 4-quart slow cooker. Cover and cook on high setting for 4 hours or until squash and leeks are tender. Carefully purée the hot soup, in 3 or 4 batches, in a food processor or blender until smooth. Add seasoned salt and white pepper. Garnish with nutmeg and sour cream. Serves 8.

slow down

Use a slow cooker for dishes that you would normally cook on the stove. Try stews, chili or even chicken and noodles. It cooks by itself, so you have a little more time with family and friends.

Turnip Greens Stew

Pull out vegetables from the freezer, and make this down-home southern stew in a snap...so yummy!

2 c. cooked ham, chopped
1 T. oil
3 c. chicken broth
1 t. sugar
1 t. seasoned pepper

2 16-oz. pkgs. frozen chopped
    turnip greens
10-oz. pkg. frozen diced onion,
    red and green bell peppers,
    and celery

Sauté ham in hot oil in a Dutch oven over medium-high heat 5 minutes or until lightly browned. Add broth and remaining ingredients; bring to a boil. Cover, reduce heat to low, and simmer, stirring occasionally, 25 minutes. Serves 6 to 8.

organize your pantry

A permanent marker makes it a snap to keep canned goods and packaged mixes rotated in the pantry. Just write the purchase date on each item as groceries are unpacked and stored.

Hearty Winter Soup

It's easy to keep the ingredients for this soup stocked in your pantry...pull them out when you need a super-quick meal.

10¾-oz. can bean soup with
   bacon
10¾-oz. can cream of potato soup
14½-oz. can stewed tomatoes,
   chopped

salt and pepper to taste
Garnish: shredded mozzarella
   cheese

   In a medium stockpot, combine soups and tomatoes; add salt and pepper. Heat until boiling; let stand several minutes before serving. Top with cheese. Serves 4 to 6.

Mary Tolliver
Welch, WV

stains no more

Spray your plastic storage containers with non-stick vegetable spray before pouring tomato-based sauces in...no stains!

Easy Potato Cheddar Soup

Warm a loaf of crusty bread to pair with this hot, bubbly soup…an easy fix on cold winter nights.

10¾-oz. can cream of potato soup
10¾-oz. can Cheddar cheese soup
3 c. milk
¼ t. salt

⅛ t. pepper
2 16-oz. cans whole potatoes, drained and diced

Combine soups, milk, salt and pepper in a large stockpot over medium heat; stir until blended. Add potatoes; simmer until hot and bubbly. Serves 6.

Sara Downing
Whitehall, OH

I keep all of the ingredients for this soup in my pantry…it can be tossed together in fifteen minutes!

Sara

Creamy Cucumber Soup

English, or hothouse, cucumbers have thin skins, few seeds, and a mild flavor.

¾ c. chicken broth
3 green onions
2 T. white vinegar
½ t. salt
¼ t. pepper
2½ lbs. English cucumbers (about 3 large), peeled, seeded and chopped

3 c. Greek yogurt
Garnish: toasted slivered almonds, additional pepper and chopped red pepper

Process chicken broth, green onions, vinegar, salt, pepper and half of chopped cucumbers in a food processor or blender until smooth, stopping to scrape down sides. Add yogurt and pulse until blended. Pour into a large bowl; stir in remaining chopped cucumbers. Cover and chill 4 to 24 hours. Garnish as desired. Makes 8 servings.

old-fashioned flair

Search out nostalgic yellowware soup tureens and matching bowls at antiques shops and auctions. They'll add vintage style to the dinner table or buffet.

Cream of Peach Soup

A sweet-tasting summer luncheon treat...pair this cool soup with a leafy green salad.

2 lbs. peaches
¼ c. sugar
1 c. water
1 c. whipping cream
½ c. white wine or apple juice

zest of 1 lemon
Garnish: chopped and sliced
    peach, fresh mint sprigs
    and chopped mint leaves

Dip peaches, one at a time, into boiling water to cover one minute. Plunge peaches immediately into ice water to stop the cooking process; drain and slip skins off. Cut peaches into quarters. Bring sugar and water to boil in a large saucepan over medium heat. Reduce heat and add peach quarters; cover and simmer 5 minutes. Cool. Process peach mixture in batches in a food processor or blender until smooth, stopping to scrape down sides. Stir together peach mixture, whipping cream, wine or apple juice, and lemon zest. Chill for 2 hours. Garnish as desired. Makes 5 servings.

Creamy Asparagus Soup

Welcome spring with a bowl of this rich and flavorful soup.

Asparagus is very plentiful in our garden in the spring, and this is a family favorite...it tastes even better the next day.

Elaine

1 to 1½ lbs. asparagus, trimmed
    and chopped
14½-oz. can chicken broth
1 T. onion, minced

1 t. salt
¼ t. white pepper
½ to ¾ c. half-and-half

    Set aside asparagus tips for garnish. Combine remaining ingredients, except half-and-half, in a stockpot over medium heat. Bring to a boil; reduce heat and simmer 5 to 7 minutes or until asparagus is tender. Ladle small batches of asparagus mixture into a food processor or blender. Add half-and-half to taste, and purée. Return mixture to stockpot, and heat through without boiling. Steam or microwave reserved asparagus tips just until tender; use to garnish soup. Serves 5.

Elaine Slabinski
Monroe Township, NJ

savory substitution

If you're out of half-and-half for a savory, summertime soup, substitute 4½ teaspoons melted butter plus enough milk to equal one cup. You also can use an equal amount of evaporated milk.

Chilled Melon Soup

This delicious and beautiful recipe is perfect for summer get-togethers with friends.

3 c. cantaloupe melon, peeled, seeded and chopped

2 T. sugar, divided

¼ c. orange juice, divided

⅛ t. salt, divided

3 c. honeydew melon, peeled, seeded and chopped

Garnish: fresh mint sprigs or orange slices

In a food processor or blender, process cantaloupe, half the sugar, half the juice and half the salt until smooth. Cover and refrigerate. Repeat with honeydew and remaining ingredients except garnish. Refrigerate, covered, in a separate container. To serve, pour equal amounts of each mixture at the same time on opposite sides of individual soup bowls. Garnish as desired. Serves 6 to 8.

Janice Woods
Northern Cambria, PA

pouring perfection

Here's a handy way to easily pour two flavors of chilled soup into a bowl at the same time. Fill two small cream pitchers with one flavor of soup each, then pour. The pitchers' small sizes make pouring so easy!

Cowboy Beef Stew

Yee-haw! Dinner's done!

5 to 6 potatoes, peeled and diced
2 carrots, peeled and thinly sliced
1 lb. ground beef
1 T. all-purpose flour
½ c. water
8-oz. can tomato sauce

Place potatoes and carrots in a saucepan; add enough water to cover vegetables by an inch. Boil gently until veggies are tender, about 30 minutes; set aside. Shape ground beef into one-inch meatballs; brown in a skillet. Add undrained vegetable mixture; heat for 5 minutes and set aside. Whisk flour and ½ cup water together in a small bowl; pour in tomato sauce. Stir into beef mixture; cover and simmer until thickened, about 15 minutes. Serves 4.

JoAngela Vassey
Cherry Hill, NJ

try kosher salt

Kosher salt has big crystals and a distinct flavor from ordinary table salt. Try it in your next recipe…just remember that one tablespoon of kosher salt is equal to 2 teaspoons of table salt.

Slow-Cooker Smoked Sausage Stew

Bake a pan of cornbread to serve alongside this filling stew.

4 to 5 potatoes, peeled and cubed
2 16-oz. cans green beans,
    undrained

1-lb. pkg. smoked sausage, sliced
1 onion, chopped
2 T. butter, sliced

Layer potatoes, green beans, sausage and onion in a slow cooker; dot with butter. Cook on low setting for 4 to 5 hours. Serves 4.

Susie Gray
Winchester, IN

soup-er easy!

Put your soup supper together the night before. Peel and chop vegetables, and store them in plastic zipping bags in the refrigerator. In the morning, simply add all soup ingredients to the slow cooker.

Chunky Tomato-
Avocado Salad,
page 116

everyday
salads &
sandwiches

Whether you're looking for a side salad or a one-dish meal, this is the chapter for you. Pair Chunky Tomato-Avocado Salad (page 116) with a south-of-the-border main dish. Or bring Spicy Peach Salad (page 135) to the next potluck. And celebrate summer with Toasted Green Tomato Sandwiches (page 136). With just five or less ingredients, all of these salads and sandwiches are a breeze to make!

Chunky Tomato-Avocado Salad

(pictured on page 114)

Let this flavorful salad sit for at least two hours if you don't have time to refrigerate it overnight.

1 avocado, pitted, peeled and cubed

3 plum tomatoes, chopped

¼ c. sweet onion, chopped

1 T. fresh cilantro, chopped

2 to 3 T. lemon juice

Gently stir together all ingredients; cover and refrigerate overnight. Serves 4.

Alma Evans
Patrick AFB, FL

make your own

Homemade croutons absorb dressing much better than store-bought. Make your own easily by cubing bread and sprinkling them with Italian seasoning and olive oil. Toast on a baking sheet at 350 degrees until crisp.

Bacon-y Romaine Salad

The savory, sweet bacon dressing makes this salad unforgettable!

2 heads romaine lettuce, chopped   1 c. cider vinegar
1 sweet onion, thinly sliced   1 c. sugar
½ lb. bacon, chopped

Arrange lettuce in a large serving bowl. Layer onion on top. Cook bacon in skillet over medium-high heat until crisp; drain. Combine vinegar and sugar; pour into skillet with bacon. Bring to a simmer over medium heat. Cook and stir vinegar mixture until sugar dissolves. Pour mixture over lettuce and onion. Toss together, and serve immediately. Serves 8.

Meredith Schaller
Watertown, WI

I serve this tasty salad alongside a grilled dinner.

Meredith

Quick & Easy Veggie Salad

A simple, healthy choice to pair with any main dish...or serve it by itself with crunchy bread.

½ head cauliflower, chopped
1 bunch broccoli, chopped
1 tomato, chopped

¼ red onion, sliced
3 to 4 T. Italian salad dressing

Combine cauliflower, broccoli, tomato and onion in a serving bowl. Toss with dressing to taste. Serves 4.

Dana Thompson
Delaware, OH

outdoor luncheon

Whether it's an afternoon with friends or a family reunion, set up a summery get-together in farmgirl style using wooden ironing boards as serving tables. Tack a clothesline around the ironing board edge, and use clothespins to secure sweet vintage hankies or dandy aprons in place.

Pepper & Corn Salad

Toss in some cherry tomatoes, sliced cucumbers or any of your favorite summer veggies.

2 15¼-oz. cans corn, drained
1 bunch green onions, chopped
1 green pepper, chopped

5-oz. jar green olives with
    pimentos, drained and sliced
1 c. Italian salad dressing

Combine all ingredients in a serving bowl; cover and chill overnight. Serves 6.

Lynn Newton
Oklahoma City, OK

summertime fun salad bar

Serve up a do-it-yourself salad bar when summer fun beckons. Alongside a large bowl of crisp greens, set out muffin tins filled with chopped veggies, diced hard-boiled eggs, grilled sliced chicken, shredded cheese and creamy dressings. A basket of hot rolls and a pitcher of icy lemonade rounds out the menu…dig in!

Cranberry-Spinach Salad

Sweet, colorful and oh-so tasty!

2 bunches spinach leaves, torn
¼ c. feta cheese, crumbled
¼ c. sweetened, dried
    cranberries

¾ c. raspberry vinaigrette salad
    dressing
¼ c. slivered almonds

Combine ingredients in a large serving bowl; toss gently. Serves 6 to 8.

Lori Wallace
Covina, CA

olive oil know-how

What kind of olive oil to use? Reserve extra-virgin olive oil for delicately flavored salad dressings and dipping sauces. The less expensive light variety is fine for cooking.

Lemony Caesar Dressing

This yummy dressing is great on more than just Caesar salads...use it to flavor poultry or fish!

½ c. olive oil
3 T. lemon juice
2 cloves garlic, minced

1 t. Dijon mustard
½ t. salt
⅛ t. pepper

Blend all ingredients until smooth. Keep refrigerated. Makes about ¾ cup.

Sandy Minten
Klamath Falls, OR

It takes just a minute to whisk together this super-fast dressing.

Sandy

Very Berry Vinaigrette

A can't-miss dressing that's yummy on spinach salad.

¼ c. olive oil
1 c. seasoned rice vinegar

10-oz. jar seedless raspberry jam

Combine all ingredients in a blender; blend until smooth. Cover and refrigerate until ready to serve. Makes about 2½ cups.

Angela Murphy
Tempe, AZ

Momma's Pea Salad

This creamy cold salad is perfect for a potluck...pass the peas please!

1 egg, hard-boiled, peeled and
    diced
15-oz. can young peas, drained

¼ c. onion, minced
¾ c. mayonnaise
1 t. garlic powder

Mix all ingredients together in a serving bowl. Cover and refrigerate overnight. Serves 6.

Sherry Shuford
Lynchburg, VA

My mom always made this salad for our family reunions in the mountains. It was the only way she could get me to eat peas!

Sherry

fresh is the best

Choose local, seasonal fresh fruits and vegetables instead of ones that have been shipped a long distance. You'll be serving your family the freshest, tastiest produce year round at the lowest prices.

Marinated Broccoli Salad

So easy...you can mix in the bag! Be sure to let the flavors blend overnight.

2 bunches broccoli flowerets,
    chopped
1 t. dill weed
¼ c. oil

¼ c. red wine vinegar
2 cloves garlic, minced
Optional: sweetened, dried
        cranberries, sliced almonds

Place ingredients in a one-gallon plastic zipping bag; close and shake well. Refrigerate overnight, shaking occasionally; serve chilled. Serves 6.

Beverly Brown
Bowie, MD

keep 'em crisp

Salad greens will stay crisp much longer if they're washed and dried as soon as they're brought home. Wrap them in paper towels to absorb moisture, and seal in a plastic zipping bag before tucking them into the crisping drawer of the refrigerator.

Country Coleslaw

Using whipping cream instead of mayonnaise gives this slaw a wonderfully creamy taste.

This recipe is from the 1940s, and it's fabulous!

Wendy

3 c. shredded cabbage
1 c. carrot, peeled and shredded
½ c. whipping cream

3 T. apple cider vinegar
salt and pepper to taste

In a large bowl, combine cabbage and carrot. In a small bowl, whip the cream and vinegar slowly. Add salt and pepper; pour over the cabbage, and toss to coat. Chill before serving. Serves 6.

Wendy Paffenroth
Pine Island, NY

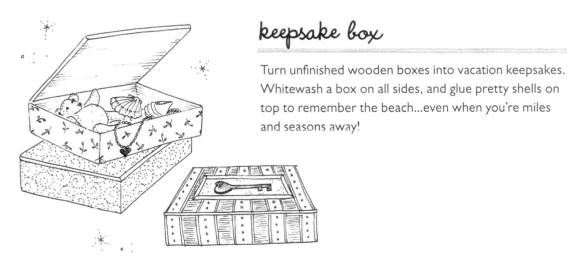

keepsake box

Turn unfinished wooden boxes into vacation keepsakes. Whitewash a box on all sides, and glue pretty shells on top to remember the beach...even when you're miles and seasons away!

Redskin Potato Salad

This is the quickest (and tastiest) potato salad ever!

8 to 10 redskin potatoes, cooked
    and chopped
2 to 3 green onions, chopped

1 to 2 c. ranch salad dressing
salt and pepper to taste

    Combine potatoes and onions in a large serving bowl. Stir in ranch dressing; season with salt and pepper. Serves 6 to 8.

Ellen Wyman
Toledo, OH

Sweet & Tangy Cucumbers

Serve these alongside sandwiches or burgers for a zing of flavor…pickled to perfection!

2 c. sugar
1 c. white vinegar
10 to 12 cucumbers, peeled and
    thinly sliced

1 to 2 onions, thinly sliced

    Whisk together sugar and vinegar until sugar is dissolved. Toss with remaining ingredients. Refrigerate until ready to serve. Serves 12 to 15.

Kathie Poritz
Burlington, WI

I used to work at a deli that served these fantastic "pickled" cucumbers…this is the secret recipe!

Kathie

Hidden Pear Salad

This classic fruity salad is so refreshing.

16-oz. can pears, drained and
    juice reserved
3-oz. pkg. lime gelatin mix
3-oz. pkg. cream cheese, softened
¼ t. lemon juice

1.3-oz. pkg. whipped
    topping mix
Garnish: whipped topping,
    lime slices

Pour pear juice into a saucepan; bring to a boil over medium heat. Remove from heat; stir in gelatin until dissolved. Set aside to cool to room temperature. Purée pears in a blender; set aside. Blend cream cheese and lemon juice until light and fluffy; mix in pears, and set aside. Prepare whipped topping according to package directions; fold into pear mixture. Add cooled gelatin; pour into an 8"x8" baking pan, and chill overnight. Garnish with whipped topping and lime slices, if desired. Serves 6 to 8.

Cindy Coffman
Lewisberry, PA

sparkling fresh fruit

For a sparkly centerpiece, brush fresh fruit and greenery with watered-down glue, then sprinkle with superfine glitter.

Mom Gowdy's Ambrosia

Ambrosia looks so pretty when served in clear glass dessert cups.

2 11-oz. cans mandarin oranges, drained
2 20-oz. cans pineapple chunks, drained
1 c. sweetened flaked coconut
2 c. sour cream
2 c. mini marshmallows

Mix all ingredients in a serving bowl; cover and refrigerate. Serves 8 to 10.

Linda Day
Wall, NJ

garden starters

After enjoying an orange or grapefruit for breakfast, don't toss the hollowed-out fruit halves. Filled with potting soil, seeds and a nice drink of water, these clever little starter plants can be planted directly in your garden!

Frozen Apricot Salad

A refreshing salad for those hot summer days.

2 12-oz. pkgs. frozen
    strawberries, thawed
12-oz. can apricot pie filling
16½-oz. can pineapple tidbits,
    drained; juice reserved

3 bananas, chopped
⅔ c. sugar

    In a large bowl, mix together all ingredients until sugar is dissolved. Pour mixture evenly into muffin cups. Place in freezer for at least 4 hours. Remove from freezer 15 minutes before serving. Serves 12.

Pat Smith
Bonham, TX

Hula Salad

Try this salad with chunks of fresh pineapple when it's in season...out-of-this-world taste!

7 c. lettuce, torn
8-oz. can pineapple chunks,
    drained and 1 T. juice reserved

1 c. shredded Cheddar cheese
½ c. mayonnaise
1 T. sugar

This salad is easy and great for any time of year.

Gretchen

    In a large bowl, toss together lettuce, pineapple and cheese; set aside. In a small bowl, combine mayonnaise, sugar and reserved pineapple juice; mix well. Pour mayonnaise mixture over salad; toss to coat. Serve immediately. Serves 6.

Gretchen Brown
Forest Grove, OR

Spicy Peach Salad

This wonderfully rich side dish includes just four ingredients.

3-oz. pkg. orange gelatin mix

29-oz. can whole spiced peaches, chopped and juice reserved

½ c. chopped pecans

8-oz. pkg. chopped dates

Prepare orange gelatin according to package directions, substituting one cup peach juice for the water; chill until slightly thickened. Fold in peaches, pecans and dates; pour into a mold or serving bowl. Chill until set. Serves 4.

Sherri Hunt
Garland, TX

handmade potpourri

Fill a wooden salad bowl with dried orange slices, dried apples and fat pine cones for a yummy smelling addition to the buffet or coffee table.

Toasted Green Tomato Sandwiches

Heat up your skillet to make this hot, buttery favorite. Tomatoes never tasted better...yum!

When my son requested these sandwiches a second time, I realized I'd "hit the mark!"

Janie

1½ to 2 c. cornmeal
salt, pepper and seasoning salt to taste
2 green tomatoes, sliced ¼-inch thick
oil or shortening for frying
2 to 3 T. butter, softened
8 slices whole-wheat bread
Optional: curly leaf lettuce, basil mayonnaise

Combine cornmeal and seasonings in a large plastic zipping bag. Shake to mix well. Add tomato slices, and gently shake to coat. Remove tomatoes from bag, shaking off excess cornmeal mixture. Heat oil or shortening in a large skillet over medium heat; fry tomatoes until golden on both sides. Remove from skillet. Spread butter on one side of each bread slice. Arrange 4 slices, butter-side down, in skillet. Cook over medium heat until toasted. Repeat with remaining bread slices. Spread mayonnaise over untoasted sides of bread, if desired. Top with tomatoes and lettuce, if desired. Close sandwich with another slice of bread. Cook sandwiches over medium heat, turning once, until golden on both sides. Serves 4.

Janie Reed
Zanesville, OH

tomato twist

Try making fried red tomatoes...a scrumptious twist on the expected green tomatoes.

Skinny Salsa Joes

The longer the beef simmers, the better these taste. Serve the mixture on toasty sandwich buns.

1 lb. ground beef, browned and
    drained
½ c. salsa

8-oz. can tomato sauce
1 T. brown sugar, packed
4 sandwich buns, split

Combine all ingredients in a saucepan except buns; bring to a boil. Reduce heat; simmer 10 to 15 minutes. Serve on buns. Serves 4.

Marcia Frahm
Urbandale, IA

sandwiches so easy

Sandwiches are a tasty solution when family members will be dining at different times. Fix sandwiches ahead of time, wrap individually, and refrigerate. Pop them into a toaster oven or under a broiler to heat...fresh, full of flavor, and ready whenever you are!

Weekend Treat Burgers

Top with sautéed mushrooms for an extra-special meal.

My husband loves big half-pound burgers, but you could make six smaller burgers if your family's appetites are lighter.

Marie

⅔ c. shredded provolone cheese
½ c. green pepper, diced
½ c. onion, chopped

salt and pepper to taste
2 lbs. ground beef chuck
4 sesame seed Kaiser rolls

Toss together cheese, green pepper, onion, salt and pepper in a large bowl. Add ground beef; mix well, and form into 4 patties. Fry in a skillet over medium-high heat for 4 to 5 minutes on each side, or until desired doneness. Serve on rolls. Serves 4.

Marie Warner
Jennings, FL

pita burgers

Tuck burgers into the pockets of halved pita rounds… easy for small hands to hold and a tasty change from the same old hamburger buns.

Excellent Burgers

Spaghetti seasoning is the secret ingredient in these juicy burgers...shh!

1 lb. lean ground beef
1 lb. ground pork
2 eggs, beaten

1½ oz. pkg. spaghetti sauce mix
8 hamburger buns, split

Combine all ingredients together except buns. Mix well, and form into 8 patties. Grill over hot coals to desired doneness. Place on buns. Serves 8.

Carrie Kelderman
Pella, IA

This recipe was created on a whim and has become a favorite! The burgers are so juicy and flavorful that we hardly need any condiments.

Carrie

Grilled Ham Panini

Treat yourself to this fast-fix sandwich on a busy night. If you don't have a bacon press, weight the sandwich with a small cast-iron skillet.

2 slices sourdough bread
1 T. mayonnaise
6 slices deli smoked ham

2 slices tomato
1 slice American cheese

Spread both slices of bread with mayonnaise on one side. Top one slice with ham, tomato, cheese and remaining bread slice. Spray a griddle or skillet with non-stick vegetable spray. Place ham sandwich on griddle; set a bacon press or other weight on top. Cook sandwich, turning once, over medium heat for about 5 minutes or until lightly golden on both sides. Makes one sandwich.

Tina Goodpasture
Meadowview, VA

Egg Salad Minis

Farm-fresh eggs are a farmers' market treat...don't pass them up!

4 eggs, hard-boiled, peeled and
    chopped
¼ c. onion, finely chopped
mayonnaise to taste, divided

salt and pepper to taste
butter to taste, softened
14 slices soft sandwich bread,
    crusts removed

Using a fork, mash eggs. Stir in onion. Add mayonnaise and salt and pepper to taste. Spread butter on half the bread slices, and spread mayonnaise on remaining bread slices. Spoon egg mixture evenly onto half of bread slices. Top with remaining bread slices, and cut diagonally into quarters. Makes 28 mini sandwiches.

Jennifer Niemi
Nova Scotia, Canada

"eggs-tra-special" sandwiches

Egg sandwiches make a super-quick and tasty meal. Scramble eggs as you like, tossing in chopped ham or shredded cheese for extra flavor. Serve on toasted, buttered English muffins alongside fresh fruit cups... ready in a flash!

Monster Meatball Sandwiches

Your family will love these dinner roll meatball sandwiches...perfect for game days.

32 bite-size frozen meatballs
9-oz. jar mango chutney
1 c. chicken broth

16 dinner rolls
16-oz. jar sweet-hot pickle
   sandwich relish

Stir together first 3 ingredients in a medium saucepan. Bring to a boil over medium-high heat. Reduce heat to low, and simmer, stirring occasionally, 25 to 30 minutes. Cut rolls vertically through top, cutting to, but not through bottom. Place 2 meatballs in each roll. Top with relish. Makes 16.

bountiful breads

Look for different kinds of breads like multi-grain, sourdough, oatmeal and marble rye...there are so many choices for tasty sandwiches!

Hot Chicken Slow-Cooker Sandwiches

Sandwiches in the slow cooker...what could be easier?

28-oz. can cooked chicken, undrained

2 10¾-oz. cans cream of chicken soup

4 T. grated Parmesan cheese

7 slices bread, toasted and cubed

24 dinner rolls

In a large bowl, combine all ingredients, except dinner rolls, and pour into a 5-quart slow cooker. Cover and cook on low setting for 3 hours. Serve on rolls. Makes 24 sandwiches.

Brenda Smith
Monroe, IN

sandwich sides

Fill up a relish tray with crunchy fresh cut-up veggies as a simple side dish for sandwiches. A creamy salad dressing can even do double duty as an easy veggie dip and a special sandwich spread.

Strawberry Patch Sandwich

Try the banana bread…it's oh-so yummy paired with peanut butter and fresh strawberries.

2 slices whole-wheat bread or
    banana bread
1 T. creamy peanut butter

1 T. cream cheese, softened
2 strawberries, hulled and sliced
1 t. honey

Spread one slice of bread with peanut butter. Spread remaining slice with cream cheese. Arrange strawberry slices in a single layer over peanut butter. Drizzle honey over berries; close sandwich. Makes one sandwich.

Shelley Turner
Boise, ID

Raspberry-Dijon Baguettes

Pair grilled chicken breasts with a tangy-sweet sauce on French bread…a masterpiece!

1 baguette, sliced
Dijon mustard to taste
raspberry jam to taste
4 boneless, skinless chicken
    breasts, grilled and sliced

2 c. arugula leaves
Optional: red onion slices

Spread 4 slices of baguette with mustard. Top remaining slices with raspberry jam. Arrange a layer of grilled chicken over mustard; top with arugula and onion, if desired. Cover with remaining baguette slices. Serves 4.

Deborah Lomax
Peoria, IL

A friend shared a similar recipe using roast beef…this is my spin on that recipe using grilled chicken.

Deborah

Baby PB&J Bagel Sandwiches

These bagels put a crunchy spin on a childhood favorite!

Sandwiches may also be cooked in a grill pan. Cook 2 minutes on each side or until lightly browned and grill marks appear.

6 mini bagels, split
6 T. creamy peanut butter

6 t. strawberry or grape jelly
1 T. butter, melted

Spread peanut butter evenly on cut sides of bottom halves of bagels; spread jelly evenly on cut sides of top halves of bagels. Place top halves of bagels on bottom halves, jelly sides down. Brush bagels lightly with melted butter; cook in a preheated panini press 2 minutes or until lightly golden and grill marks appear. Serve immediately. Serves 6.

Sweet Smoky Sandwiches

Add pizzazz to the common turkey sandwich with a sour apple and honey-nut cream cheese spread.

2 Granny Smith apples, cored
     and cut into thin slices
2 T. lemon juice
½ c. honey nut cream cheese

8 whole grain bread slices
¾ lb. deli smoked turkey breast,
     sliced thin

Toss apple slices with lemon juice; drain. Spread cream cheese evenly on one side of each bread slice; top 4 slices of bread evenly with apple slices and turkey. Cover with remaining bread slices, cream cheese side down. Makes 4.

Baby PB&J Bagel Sandwiches

Spring Spinach Sauté,
page 152

sides

so easy

Stop your side-dish search and start cooking! Make family favorites like Corny Macaroni Casserole (page 154) or Weda's Stuffed Tomatoes (page 158). Jazz up the same old standbys with Toasty Green Beans & Walnuts (page 187) or Green Chile Rice (page 156). These pages are bursting with easy-to-create sides to go with any main dish.

Spring Spinach Sauté

(pictured on page 150)

This delicious vegetarian dish is also great with pork chops.

1 to 2 cloves garlic, minced
2 T. olive oil
6-oz. pkg. baby spinach

½ c. feta cheese, crumbled
¼ c. slivered almonds

Sauté garlic in hot oil until golden; add spinach leaves, stirring until crisp-tender. Add feta cheese and almonds; heat through. Serves 4.

Beth Childers
Urbana, OH

jump-start your garden

Start cool weather veggies like lettuce and spinach indoors in old wooden drawers, and get a jump-start on the garden! Just line drawers with plastic, add gravel for drainage, and plant away. The plants can go directly outside once the days warm up.

Saucy Zucchini & Tomatoes

Serve with crusty bread and a tall glass of icy sweet tea for a delightfully simple lunch.

2 T. bacon drippings
1 onion, sliced
1 c. tomatoes, chopped

½ bay leaf
salt and pepper to taste
3 zucchini, sliced 1-inch thick

Heat drippings in a skillet over medium heat. Add onion; sauté until translucent. Add tomatoes, bay leaf, salt and pepper; simmer for 5 minutes. Add zucchini; cover and simmer until tender, about 8 to 10 minutes. Discard bay leaf before serving. Serves 4 to 6.

Gerry Donnella
Boston, VA

Remember this recipe when you have a bumper crop of zucchini in your garden this year!
Gerry

stacking skillets

Protect non-stick skillets from scratching when stacked in a cupboard…slip a paper plate or coffee filter in between them.

Corny Macaroni Casserole

Two favorite side dishes combine to make one outstanding casserole!

I like to double this recipe for a yummy potluck dish.

Deb

1 c. elbow macaroni, uncooked
15¼-oz. can corn
14¾-oz. can creamed corn

1 c. pasteurized process cheese
 spread, cubed
½ c. butter, melted

Mix together all ingredients; transfer to a greased 2-quart casserole dish. Cover and bake at 350 degrees for 40 minutes. Uncover and bake for an additional 20 minutes. Serves 4 to 6.

Deb Blean
Morrison, IL

homemade white sauce

Turn cooked veggies or macaroni into a creamy side dish with a quick homemade white sauce. Melt 2 tablespoons butter in a saucepan over low heat. Whisk in 2 tablespoons all-purpose flour until smooth, then add 2 cups milk. Cook and stir until thickened; stir in veggies or macaroni. Add salt and pepper to taste, and serve.

Green Chile Rice

Sprinkle with diced jalapeño peppers for an extra kick!

4 c. cooked rice
8-oz. pkg. shredded mozzarella
    cheese

2 c. sour cream
4-oz. can diced green chiles,
    drained

Combine all ingredients in a bowl and mix well. Pour into an ungreased 2-quart casserole dish. Bake, uncovered, at 400 degrees until bubbly, about 20 minutes. Serves 6.

Debbie Wilson
Weatherford, TX

rice done right

For extra-fluffy white rice, just add a teaspoon of white vinegar to the cooking water.

Weda's Stuffed Tomatoes

Tasty with a broiled steak or fried chicken.

10 roma tomatoes, halved
   lengthwise
½ c. shredded mozzarella cheese
½ c. crumbled feta cheese

1 T. olive oil
pepper to taste
Optional: bread crumbs

    Scoop out insides of tomato halves. Mix together cheeses, and carefully spoon into tomatoes. Arrange tomatoes in a lightly greased 13"x9" baking pan. Drizzle oil over tomatoes; sprinkle with pepper and bread crumbs, if desired. Bake, uncovered, at 375 degrees for 15 to 20 minutes. Serves 10.

Weda Mosellie
Phillipsburg, NJ

Green Tomato Casserole

Pepper Jack cheese and mild banana peppers add a spicy kick to this summer casserole.

1½ sleeves round buttery crackers, crushed and divided

3 to 4 green tomatoes, sliced ¼-inch thick and divided

16-oz. jar mild banana peppers, drained and divided

8-oz. pkg. shredded Pepper Jack cheese, divided

2 T. butter, diced

Arrange half the cracker crumbs in a 13"x9" baking pan sprayed with non-stick vegetable spray. Arrange a layer of green tomato slices on top of crumbs. Top tomatoes with half the banana peppers and half the cheese. Repeat layering again. Top with remaining cracker crumbs and butter. Bake, covered, at 325 degrees for one hour. Uncover and bake for an additional 30 minutes. Serves 12 to 15.

Hollie Kouns
Ashland, KY

plan ahead

Making your favorite casserole? Make an extra one to freeze, and enjoy it the next time you need a quick dinner!

Spicy Carrot French Fries

The sweet flavor that comes from roasting root vegetables mixed with the spicy seasonings is unusual and delicious.

2 lbs. carrots, peeled and cut into matchsticks
4 T. olive oil, divided
1 T. seasoned salt

2 t. ground cumin
1 t. chili powder
1 t. pepper
ranch salad dressing

Place carrots in a plastic zipping bag. Sprinkle with 3 tablespoons oil and seasonings; toss to coat. Drizzle remaining oil over a baking sheet; place carrots in a single layer on sheet. Bake, uncovered, at 425 degrees for 25 to 35 minutes, until carrots are golden. Serve with salad dressing for dipping. Serves 4 to 6.

Kelly Gray
Weston, WV

My children didn't know until they were almost grown that this dish was healthy for you, or even that it was a vegetable!

Kelly

sweet potato fries

Sweet potato fries are deliciously different! Slice sweet potatoes into strips or wedges, toss with olive oil, and place on a baking sheet. Bake at 400 degrees for 20 to 40 minutes until tender, turning once. Sprinkle with a little cinnamon sugar for added sweetness or chili powder for a spicy kick.

Simple Scalloped Tomatoes

This tangy-sweet side is delicious with fish and seafood.

1 onion, chopped
¼ c. butter
28-oz. can diced tomatoes
5 slices bread, lightly toasted and
    cubed

¼ c. brown sugar, packed
½ t. salt
¼ t. pepper

Cook onion in butter until just tender, but not browned. Combine onion mixture with tomatoes and their juice in a bowl; add remaining ingredients, and mix well. Pour into a greased 8"x8" baking pan. Bake, uncovered, at 350 degrees for 45 minutes. Serves 4 to 6.

Joan White
Malvern, PA

This is a scrumptious way to prepare canned tomatoes...don't be tempted to substitute fresh tomatoes!

Joan

fantastic frozen veggies

Don't hesitate to stock up on frozen vegetables when they go on sale. Flash-frozen soon after harvesting, they actually retain more nutrients than fresh produce that has traveled for several days before arriving in the grocery store's produce aisle.

Broccoli with Lemon Sauce

Lemon-lime soda spruces up steamed broccoli.

Everyone begs me to bring this dish to family gatherings.

Janet

1 bunch broccoli, chopped
1 T. lemon juice

1 T. lemon-lime soda

In a large saucepan, cover broccoli with water; simmer for 12 minutes, and drain. Mix lemon juice and lemon-lime soda; spoon over broccoli. Keep warm until ready to serve. Serves 4.

Janet Pastrick
Struthers, OH

try store brands

Give store brands a try for canned veggies, soups, sauces, boxed baking mixes and other pantry staples! You'll find they usually taste just as good as famous-label items and save you money, too.

Cheesy Cauliflower

Use spicy brown mustard for a bold flavor!

1¼ t. mayonnaise
1¼ t. mustard
1 head cauliflower, chopped
    and cooked

¼ c. butter, sliced
¾ c. grated Parmesan cheese

In a small bowl, combine mayonnaise and mustard. Place cauliflower in an ungreased 2-quart baking dish; spread with mustard mixture, and dot with butter. Sprinkle with cheese. Bake, uncovered, at 375 degrees for 30 minutes. Serves 4 to 6.

John Alexander
New Britain, CT

Italian Green Beans

These beans are delicious with chicken, steak, or just about anything.

2 14½-oz. cans green beans
½ c. Italian salad dressing

1 t. Italian seasoning

Place beans in a medium saucepan; stir in salad dressing and seasoning. Bring to a boil over medium heat; turn down to a simmer. Cook, stirring occasionally, until most of liquid is gone. Serves 4.

Amy Lynn Boswell
Xenia, OH

I decided to try something new one evening. Now this is my husband Chad's favorite way to eat green beans!

Amy Lynn

Cinnamon-Apple Noodle Bake

A delicious and unusual side dish for pork chops.

2 c. medium egg noodles,
    uncooked
3 T. butter, divided

4 apples, peeled, cored and sliced
¾ c. sugar
1 t. cinnamon

Cook noodles according to package directions. Melt 2 tablespoons butter, and spread in a 2½-quart casserole dish. Layer half the cooked noodles in dish, and top with all the apples; set aside. Mix sugar and cinnamon; sprinkle half over apples. Top with remaining noodles. Dot with remaining butter, and sprinkle with remaining sugar mixture. Bake, uncovered, at 350 degrees for 35 to 40 minutes. Serves 6 to 8.

Dorothy Brandt
Avon, SD

best pie apples

For the best pie apples, count on Jonathan, Winesap, Braeburn, Fuji, Rome Beauty, Granny Smith and Pippin apples.

Homestyle Butterbeans

Use this recipe for lima beans, too!

5 bacon slices, diced

1 onion, minced

½ c. brown sugar, packed

16-oz. pkg. frozen butterbeans

¼ c. butter

12 c. water

2 t. salt

1 t. pepper

Cook bacon and onion in a large Dutch oven over medium heat 5 to 7 minutes. Add brown sugar, and cook, stirring occasionally, one to 2 minutes or until sugar is dissolved. Stir in butterbeans and butter until butter is melted and beans are thoroughly coated. Stir in water. Bring to a boil over medium-high heat; reduce heat to low. Simmer, stirring occasionally, 2 hours or until beans are very tender and liquid is thickened and just below top of beans. Stir in salt and pepper. Serves 6 to 8.

tasty veggie plate

Serve up a veggie plate for dinner...a good old southern tradition. With 2 or 3 scrumptious veggie dishes and a basket of buttery cornbread, no one will miss the meat!

Cheesy Ranch Potatoes

Try a different seasoning mix to create another flavorful take on ordinary mashed potatoes.

Traditional potatoes with a cheesy twist!

Dayna

4-oz. pkg. buttermilk ranch salad dressing mix
1 c. buttermilk
1 c. sour cream

6 to 8 potatoes, boiled and chopped
3 c. shredded Cheddar cheese, divided

In a small bowl, combine dressing mix with buttermilk and sour cream. In a large bowl, combine potatoes, 2 cups of cheese and dressing mixture. Pour potato mixture into an ungreased 13"x9" baking pan. Top with remaining cheese. Bake, uncovered, at 350 degrees for 25 to 30 minutes. Serves 8 to 10.

Dayna Hansen
Junction City, OR

no-fuss shepherd's pie

For a mock shepherd's pie in minutes, just substitute a can of cream of celery soup and frozen hashbrowns for the mashed potatoes…less fuss and just as tasty!

Minted Baby Carrots

Mint is so easy to grow…keep some growing in a sunny spot by the kitchen door, and you can whip up these yummy carrots anytime.

½ lb. baby carrots	1 T. lemon zest, minced
2 T. butter	1 T. brown sugar, packed
salt and pepper to taste	2 t. fresh mint, minced

In a stockpot of boiling water, cook carrots 5 minutes. Remove from heat, and drain. Melt butter in a skillet over medium-high heat. Stir in carrots; cook until crisp-tender. Season with salt and pepper to taste. Combine remaining ingredients, and sprinkle over individual servings. Serves 4.

Tori Willis
Champaign, IL

fresh from the market

Farmers' market foods taste so fresh because they're all grown and picked in season at the peak of flavor… lettuce, asparagus and strawberries in the springtime, tomatoes, peppers and sweet corn in the summer, and squash and greens in the fall and winter.

Vidalia Onion Side Dish

Onion-lovers will rave over this tasty side item cooked in the microwave in minutes.

2 Vidalia onions
2 cubes beef bouillon

1 T. butter
Optional: fresh parsley, pepper

Peel onions, and cut a thin slice from bottom and top of each one. Scoop out a one-inch-deep hole from the top of each onion. Place onions, top sides up, in a 2-quart microwave-safe dish with a lid. Add one bouillon cube and ½ tablespoon butter to shallow hole in each onion. Microwave, covered, on high for 8 to 10 minutes or until onion is tender. Garnish with fresh parsley and pepper, if desired. Serves 2.

Try grilling the onions wrapped in heavy-duty aluminum foil for about 12 to 15 minutes. Be sure to use only Vidalia or Texas Sweet onions.

Fried Pecan Okra

You can use a 16-ounce package of frozen cut okra, thawed, if you'd rather have bite-size pieces.

1 c. pecans
1½ c. biscuit baking mix
1 t. salt
½ t. pepper

2 10-oz. pkgs. frozen whole
   okra, thawed
peanut oil

    Place pecans in an even layer in a shallow pan. Bake at 350 degrees for 10 minutes or until lightly toasted, stirring occasionally. Process pecans, baking mix, and salt and pepper in a food processor until nuts are finely ground. Place pecan mixture in a large bowl. Add okra, tossing to coat. Gently press pecan mixture into okra. Pour oil to a depth of 2 inches into a Dutch oven or cast-iron skillet; heat to 350 degrees. Fry okra, in batches, turning once, for 5 to 6 minutes, until golden; drain on paper towels. Serves 6 to 8.

sweet-smelling sponges

Keep kitchen sponges smelling lemony fresh! Soak them in lemon juice, then rinse well with clear water.

Pronto Refried Beans

A sprinkle of queso fresco, a fresh white Mexican cheese, adds traditional flavor to this quick side dish. You can buy it at your local supercenter or Hispanic market.

14½-oz. can stewed
   Mexican-style tomatoes
31-oz. can refried beans
1 t. chili powder

½ t. cumin
4 oz. queso fresco, crumbled
Optional: fresh cilantro

Stir together tomatoes, refried beans, chili powder cumin. Transfer to a lightly greased 2-quart baking dish. Sprinkle evenly with queso fresco. Bake, uncovered, at 350 degrees for 25 minutes or until thoroughly heated. Let stand 5 minutes before serving. Garnish with cilantro, if desired. Serves 6.

take two!

Fix a double batch! Brown two pounds of ground beef with two packages of taco seasoning mix, then freeze half of the mixture for a quick meal of tacos or taco salad another night.

Creamy Italian Noodles

These zesty noodles are so quick and easy to prepare...a super alternative to rice or potatoes.

8-oz. pkg. thin egg noodles, uncooked
¼ c. butter, sliced
½ c. evaporated milk or half-and-half

¼ c. grated Parmesan cheese
2¼ t. Italian salad dressing mix

In a saucepan, cook egg noodles according to package directions; drain and set aside. In the same saucepan, melt butter. Return noodles to pan, and add milk or half-and-half and cheese. Stir to combine; add dressing mix, and stir again. Serves 4.

Beth Shaeffer
Greenwood, IN

microwave steaming

Steam crisp-tender vegetables in the microwave. Place cut-up veggies in a microwave-safe container, and add a little water. Cover with plastic wrap, venting with a knife tip. Microwave on high for 2 to 5 minutes, checking for tenderness after each minute. Uncover carefully to allow hot steam to escape.

Crispy Baked Eggplant

Serve with warm marinara sauce.

2 T. oil
1 eggplant, sliced ½-inch thick

2 eggs, beaten
1 c. biscuit baking mix

Brush oil over a baking sheet; set aside. Dip eggplant slices into eggs, and coat with baking mix; arrange on baking sheet. Bake at 375 degrees on top rack of oven for 15 minutes; turn over, and bake an additional 15 minutes until golden and tender. Serves 4.

Phyllis Peters
Three Rivers, MI

Corn for a Crowd

This creamy side is a number one choice for your next potluck dinner... plenty to go around!

5-lb. pkg. frozen corn
2 8-oz. pkgs. cream cheese,
    cubed and softened

½ c. sweetened condensed milk

This side dish is a real crowd-pleaser!

Bonnie

Cook corn according to package directions; stir in cream cheese until melted. Drizzle milk on top; mix well. Serves 10 to 15.

Bonnie Huckabee
San Angelo, TX

Browned Butter Mashed Potatoes

Try tossing browned butter with steamed vegetables, or drizzle it over warm, crusty French bread.

¾ c. butter
4 lbs. Yukon gold potatoes, peeled
    and cut into 2-inch pieces
1 T. salt, divided
¾ c. buttermilk

½ c. milk
¼ t. pepper
Optional: fresh parsley,
    rosemary and thyme sprigs

Cook butter in a heavy saucepan over medium heat, stirring constantly, 6 to 8 minutes or just until butter begins to turn golden brown. Immediately remove from heat and pour butter into a small bowl. Remove and reserve one to 2 tablespoons browned butter. Place potatoes in a Dutch oven; cover with water and add salt. Bring to a boil; boil over medium-high heat for 20 minutes, or until potatoes are tender. Drain. Reduce heat to low. Return potatoes to Dutch oven, and cook, stirring occasionally, 3 to 5 minutes or until potatoes are dry. Mash potatoes with a potato masher to desired consistency. Add remaining ingredients except reserved one to 2 tablespoons butter and fresh herbs; stir just until blended. Transfer to a serving dish. Drizzle with reserved browned butter. Garnish, if desired. Serves 6 to 8.

herbed new potatoes

Buttery herbed potatoes are satisfying and quick to fix. Choose the smallest new potatoes so they'll cook quickly in boiling water. Once potatoes are tender, toss them with butter and snipped fresh chives and parsley.

Golden Rice Bake

A yummy side for grilled sausage, hot dogs or chicken.

5-oz. pkg. saffron yellow rice, cooked

10¾-oz. can cream of mushroom soup

11-oz. can sweet corn and diced peppers, drained

½ c. butter, melted

Mix all ingredients well. Spoon into a greased 1½-quart casserole dish. Bake, uncovered, at 350 degrees for 20 minutes, until hot and bubbly. Serves 4.

Angela Lively
Baxter, TN

steamed rice secret

The secret to tender steamed rice: Cook long-cooking rice according to package directions. When it's done, remove pan from heat, cover with a folded tea towel, and put the lid back on. Let stand for 5 to 10 minutes before serving. The towel will absorb any excess moisture.

Bacon-Brown Sugar Brussels Sprouts

A delicious way to have your family eating this leafy veggie!

4 slices bacon
14-oz. can chicken broth
1 T. brown sugar, packed

1 t. salt
1½ lbs. Brussels sprouts,
   trimmed and halved

   Cook bacon in a Dutch oven over medium heat 10 minutes or until crisp. Remove bacon, and drain on paper towels, reserving drippings in Dutch oven. Crumble bacon. Add broth, brown sugar and salt to drippings in Dutch oven, and bring to a boil. Stir in Brussels sprouts. Cover and cook 6 to 8 minutes or until tender. Transfer to a serving bowl using a slotted spoon, and sprinkle with bacon. Serve immediately. Serves 6 to 8.

say it with sprouts

Uncooked Brussels sprouts make clever placecard holders! Slice the bottom off each so they sit flat, then cut a slit in the tops to hold name cards.

Kristen's Baked Beans

Humble ingredients combine to make old-fashioned goodness. Include these beans at your next barbecue.

Worthy of grandma's hand-me-down bean pot.

Kristen

15-oz. can pork and beans
1 t. mustard
1 T. dried, minced onion
¼ c. catsup
¼ c. brown sugar, packed

Combine all ingredients; mix well, and pour into a greased 8"x8" baking dish. Bake, uncovered, at 350 degrees for 30 minutes. Serves 4.

Kristen Lewis
Bourbonnais, IL

Maple Sweet Potatoes

Sweet and yummy! The apples are a surprising touch.

1 t. vanilla extract
1 c. maple syrup
3 T. butter
4 to 5 red apples, peeled, cored
    and sliced
4 to 5 sweet potatoes, boiled,
    peeled and sliced

Simmer vanilla extract and maple syrup in a large saucepan for 5 to 10 minutes; add butter and apples. Cook until the apples are fork tender; remove from sauce with a slotted spoon. In a greased 2-quart casserole dish, layer apples and potatoes; pour sauce mixture over all. Bake, covered, at 325 degrees for 20 minutes. Serves 6.

Wendy Paffenroth
Pine Island, NY

Toasty Green Beans & Walnuts

If you want, replace the shallots with green onions (using the white part only) and a bit of minced garlic.

24-oz. can green beans, drained	2 shallots, sliced
½ c. chopped walnuts	¼ t. salt
1 T. olive oil	¼ t. pepper

Place beans in a medium saucepan. Add lightly salted water to cover; simmer over medium heat for 5 minutes. Drain and cool. Place nuts in a dry non-stick skillet over medium-low heat. Cook and stir for about 3 minutes until toasted. Set aside nuts. Heat oil in same skillet; add shallots, and sauté for 5 minutes until soft. Add green beans, nuts, salt and pepper; toss over medium heat for 2 to 3 minutes. Serves 6.

Jan Frazier
Louisville, KY

bring out the flavor

Toasting really brings out the flavor of shelled nuts…
and it's oh-so-easy! Place nuts in a small dry skillet.
Cook and stir over low heat for a few minutes until
the nuts are toasty and golden.

Slow-Cooker Creamy
Apricot Chicken, page 196

main dish
mainstays

With just a few ingredients…and these recipes…you can have a marvelous meal! Get started tonight by serving Saucy Pork Chops (page 197) or Sour Cream Chicken Rolls (page 195). Looking for a one-dish supper? Try Family Favorite Chili Mac (page 207), Chicken & Wild Rice (page 198), or Cheeseburger Bake (page 234). From now on, suppertime will be a cinch!

Garlicky Chicken & Redskin Potatoes

Roasted chicken with veggies fresh from the farmers' market...what could be better?

Our farmers' market runs from May through the end of October. Vendors have tables filled with fresh-baked goods, flowers, fruit, veggies, herbs, perennials and honey. There's something for everyone to enjoy!

Vickie

8 chicken breasts
3 lbs. redskin potatoes, halved
20 cloves garlic, peeled
1 T. fresh thyme, chopped

salt and pepper to taste
¼ c. olive oil
Optional: fresh thyme sprigs

Place chicken in an ungreased roasting pan. Arrange potatoes and garlic around chicken. Sprinkle with seasonings, and drizzle with oil. Bake, uncovered, at 425 degrees for 20 minutes. Reduce oven temperature to 375 degrees. Continue baking 45 minutes to one hour or until chicken is golden and juices run clear. Transfer chicken to a platter. Spoon potatoes and garlic around edges. Garnish with thyme sprigs, if desired. Serves 8.

Vickie
Gooseberry Patch

growing garlic

While you're at the farmers' market, pick up a garlic bulb to plant in your own garden. (Don't use regular supermarket garlic, which was probably treated with a sprouting inhibitor.) Plant individual cloves two inches deep and one foot apart. When flower stalks begin to appear, cut them back. About midsummer, the leaves will begin to turn yellow...time to dig up your garlic and enjoy!

Easy Gumbo Meatballs

After baking, keep these warm in a slow cooker...they're a potluck favorite!

2 lbs. ground beef
4 slices bread, crumbled
¾ c. evaporated milk

10¾-oz. can chicken gumbo soup
10½-oz. can French onion soup
Optional: fresh parsley

Combine first 3 ingredients together; form into one-inch balls. Arrange in an ungreased 13"x9" baking pan; pour soups on top. Bake, uncovered, at 350 degrees for 1½ hours. Serve over cooked rice. Garnish with parsley, if desired. Serves 6.

Brenda Flowers
Olney, IL

paint to perfection

Vintage glass milk bottles and vases can be dressed up with paint...many craft paints are made just for glass. Add festive polka dots and stripes in old-fashioned colors, or create a whimsical checkerboard.

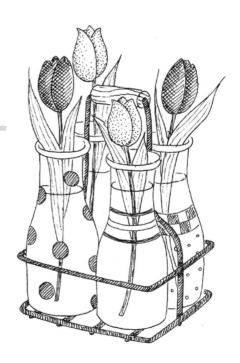

Sour Cream Chicken Rolls

Impress your guests with this entrée, and they'll keep coming back for more! It is simple, yummy, and makes a nice presentation.

4 boneless, skinless chicken breasts
16-oz. container sour cream

6-oz. pkg. stuffing mix, crushed
6-oz. pkg. long-grain and wild rice, cooked

Place chicken breasts between 2 pieces of plastic wrap; pound to flatten slightly. Brush sour cream over chicken, coating both sides well. Dip into stuffing mix, coating both sides. Discard any remaining stuffing mix. Roll up chicken; secure each roll with a toothpick. Place in a 9"x9" baking pan that has been sprayed with non-stick vegetable spray; cover with aluminum foil. Bake at 350 degrees for 30 minutes. Remove foil; bake for another 15 minutes or until chicken is cooked through. Slice rolls across into spirals. Serve over cooked rice. Serves 4.

Joanne Wilson
Roselle Park, NJ

My friend shared this recipe with me many years ago. I still request it whenever she asks me over for dinner. The chicken even makes a delicious cold sandwich the next day...give it a try!

Joanne

flatten 'em first!

Boneless chicken and pork slices cook up tender in a jiffy if they're flattened first. Get a rubber mallet from the hardware store just for this purpose. Its soft surface won't tear the wax paper or plastic wrap like a metal meat mallet will.

Sweet & Spicy Chicken

With four simple ingredients, this marinated chicken is great for springtime cookouts.

½ c. orange juice
¼ c. honey
1-oz. env. Italian salad
    dressing mix

6 boneless, skinless chicken
    breasts

Mix first 3 ingredients together; add chicken breasts. Marinate for one hour, turning to coat both sides. Grill or broil until juices run clear when chicken is pierced with a fork. Serves 6.

Joan Sumner
Callao, VA

Slow-Cooker Creamy Apricot Chicken
(pictured on page 188)

Serve with creamy mashed potatoes and your favorite veggie. Then pour on spoonfuls of the creamy apricot sauce.

8-oz. bottle Russian salad
    dressing
12-oz. jar apricot preserves

1 to 2 lbs. boneless, skinless
    chicken breasts

Combine salad dressing and preserves together; set aside. Arrange chicken in a 5-quart slow cooker; pour dressing mixture on top. Cover and cook on high setting for 1 hour, then on low setting for 3 hours or until done. Serves 4 to 6.

Tami Hoffman
Litchfield, NH

Crispy Pork Cutlets

Crispy and tender, these cutlets go well with sweet potatoes or wild rice.

2 eggs
2 T. mustard
2 lbs. pork cutlets

1 c. instant mashed potato flakes
3 T. oil

Blend eggs and mustard together in a shallow pie pan; set aside. Dip pork cutlets in egg mixture; coat with potato flakes. Heat oil in a skillet; add pork, cooking 2 minutes on each side until golden and cooked through. Serves 4 to 6.

Patricia Roisum
Marshall, WI

Saucy Pork Chops

You'll want to finish every drop of the delicious sauce!

2 10¾-oz. cans cream of
   chicken soup
½ c. catsup

6 t. Worcestershire sauce
4 to 6 pork chops
2½ c. cooked rice

This saucy bake works well with chicken, too!

Cindy

Mix together soup, catsup and Worcestershire sauce; set aside. Arrange pork chops in an ungreased 13"x9" baking pan; pour soup mixture over the top. Cover and bake at 350 degrees for one hour. Serve each pork chop on a serving of rice; spoon remaining sauce on top. Serves 4 to 6.

Cindy McCormick
Bakersfield, CA

Chicken & Wild Rice

Mmmm…great with fresh-baked bread and a green salad.

2 6.2-oz. pkgs. quick-cooking
   long-grain and wild rice with
   seasoning packets
4 boneless, skinless chicken
   breasts, cut into 1" cubes

10¾-oz. can cream of
   mushroom soup
1⅓ c. frozen mixed
   vegetables, thawed
3 c. water

Gently stir together all ingredients. Spread into an ungreased 13"x9" baking pan. Bake, uncovered, at 350 degrees until juices run clear when chicken is pierced with a fork, about 45 minutes, stirring occasionally. Serves 6 to 8.

Kimberly Lyons
Commerce, TX

Slow-Cooker Sweet & Spicy Country-Style Ribs

Serve with coleslaw and crusty bread for a perfect picnic dinner.

My husband, Randy, and I made up this recipe for our slow cooker because we love barbecued ribs.

Kandy

2 to 3 lbs. country-style bone-in
   pork ribs
1 onion, sliced
salt and pepper to taste

18-oz. bottle barbecue sauce
½ c. maple syrup
¼ c. spicy brown mustard

Place ribs in a 6-quart oval slow cooker that has been sprayed with non-stick vegetable spray. Place onion on top of ribs; sprinkle with salt and pepper. Mix together remaining ingredients; pour on top of ribs. Cover and cook on low setting for 8 to 10 hours. Serves 4 to 6.

Kandy Bingham
Green River, WY

Chicken & Wild Rice

Poor Man's Cordon Bleu

Poor Man's Cordon Bleu

A quick and easy variation on a classic.

16 slices deli turkey
8 slices deli ham
16 slices Swiss cheese

½ c. water
2 c. Italian-flavored dry bread
    crumbs, divided

A great dish for a
weekend lunch, too!

Linda

For each turkey roll, lay out 2 turkey slices, overlapping ends by
2 to 3 inches. Add a ham slice, centered on turkey slices. Place 2 cheese
slices on top, with ends barely touching. Roll up, starting on one short
side. Repeat with remaining ingredients to make 8 rolls. Dip rolls into
water to dampen, and coat in bread crumbs, reserving ¼ cup bread
crumbs for topping. Place rolls seam-side down in a greased 13"x9"
baking pan. Sprinkle reserved crumbs on top. Bake, uncovered, at
350 degrees for 15 to 20 minutes until lightly golden and cheese is
melted. Serves 4.

Linda Lamb
Round Rock, TX

Chicken Pot Pie

The easiest and tastiest pot pie you'll ever make!

2 to 3-lb. deli roast chicken,
    shredded or chopped
10¾-oz. can cream of
    mushroom soup with garlic
16-oz. pkg. frozen mixed
    vegetables, thawed

2 stalks celery, chopped
12-oz. tube refrigerated dinner
    rolls

My son, Frankie,
loves to help make
this for dinner.

Kate

Mix together chicken, soup, vegetables and celery. Spoon into a
lightly greased 9"x9" baking pan. Separate and flatten rolls; place on
top of mixture. Bake, uncovered, at 350 degrees for 25 minutes or until
bubbly and rolls are golden. Serves 4.

Kate Kelly Gallegos
Aurora, IL

Quick & Easy Lasagna

Extra cheesy, this lasagna's a winner!

1 lb. ground beef, browned
2 24-oz. jars pasta sauce
16-oz. pkg. lasagna noodles,
    cooked and divided

2 c. ricotta cheese, divided
16-oz. pkg. shredded mozzarella
    cheese, divided

Mix together ground beef and pasta sauce; set aside. Spread 1 cup pasta sauce mixture on the bottom of an ungreased 13"x9" baking pan; layer with about half the noodles. Pour half the sauce on top; drop half the ricotta cheese by spoonfuls onto the sauce. Sprinkle with half the mozzarella cheese; repeat layers, beginning with noodles. Bake, uncovered, at 350 degrees for 30 to 35 minutes or until cheese melts. Serves 12.

Tina Stuart
Scottsdale, AZ

kitchen luminaries

Fill the tiniest terra cotta pots with votive candles. Lined up on a windowsill, they'll add a warm and cozy glow to any kitchen!

Salmon Delight

A simple and delicious recipe for fish lovers.

Here in Alaska we
really know our salmon.
This is a very simple
baked recipe that
is out of this world...
I guarantee that
it's delicious!

Carol

1½-lb. salmon fillet
2 T. butter, melted
1 c. mayonnaise

14 round buttery crackers,
    crushed

Pat salmon dry with a paper towel. Spread butter in a 13"x9" baking pan; place salmon in pan skin-side down. Spread mayonnaise over salmon in a thin layer; sprinkle with cracker crumbs until well coated. Bake, uncovered, at 350 degrees for about 20 minutes or until crumbs turn golden. Slice into serving portions. Serves 4.

Carol Dreeszen
King Salmon, AK

Chicken Spaghetti Pie

A family-pleasing way to turn leftover spaghetti and chicken into a second yummy meal.

I like to use already
seasoned sauce for an
extra flavor boost.

Barb

3 c. cooked spaghetti
1½ c. cooked chicken, diced
1 c. pasteurized process cheese
    spread, cubed

15-oz. can pizza or tomato sauce
Garnish: grated Parmesan cheese

In a bowl, combine all ingredients except Parmesan cheese. Mix well; press mixture into a lightly greased 9" round pie plate. Sprinkle with Parmesan cheese. Bake, uncovered, at 400 degrees for 15 to 20 minutes until heated through. Let stand for 5 minutes before cutting into wedges. Serves 4.

Barb Stout
Gooseberry Patch

Speedy Stroganoff

Your family will ask for seconds when this tasty skillet supper is on the menu!

1 lb. ground beef
1 onion, diced
2 t. paprika
1 t. salt
½ t. pepper
10¾-oz. can cream of mushroom
   soup
16-oz. container sour cream
cooked egg noodles

In a skillet over medium heat, brown beef and onion; drain. Add paprika, salt and pepper, stirring in thoroughly. Reduce heat to medium-low; blend in soup, and heat through. Stir in sour cream and cook just until warmed through. Serve over cooked noodles. Serves 4.

Connie Ferrell
Blanchester, OH

Mandarin Pork Chops

The spicy citrus aroma of these simmering chops will beckon your guests to the table.

4 to 6 pork chops
1 T. oil
11-oz. can mandarin oranges,
   drained
½ t. ground cloves
⅛ t. pepper

In a large skillet, brown pork chops in hot oil for 3 to 5 minutes per side. Top with oranges; sprinkle with cloves and pepper. Cover and cook over medium heat for 15 minutes or until juices run clear. Serves 4 to 6.

Susan Young
Madison, AL

A terrific dinner party recipe...it's simple and quick but tastes like you spent hours on it.

Susan

Family Favorite Chili Mac

Kids love this quick and easy dinner. Serve with a tossed salad and cornbread sticks.

2 7¼-oz. pkgs. macaroni & cheese, uncooked
10-oz. can diced tomatoes and green chiles
1 to 2 lbs. ground beef
1¼-oz. pkg. taco seasoning mix
chili powder, salt and pepper to taste

Prepare macaroni and cheese according to package directions. Stir in tomatoes and green chiles; set aside. Brown beef in a skillet; drain and mix in taco seasoning. Stir beef mixture into macaroni mixture. Add seasonings as desired; heat through. Serves 7 to 9.

Stephanie McNealy
Talala, OK

freezing extra pasta

So often there's extra cooked macaroni or pasta left over. It's fine to freeze it for later. Drain well, toss with a little oil, and freeze in a plastic zipping bag. To reuse, place the frozen pasta in a colander, rinse it with hot water to separate, and stir the pasta into a skillet or casserole dish. Heat until warmed through.

Right after my husband and I were married, we were living on a tight budget. One weekend our cupboard was so bare that I just started tossing food into pots and hoping for something tasty to happen. My husband, his kids, and our new little girl sure love this very inexpensive dish... thank goodness!

Stephanie

Savory Cranberry Chicken

Perfect for a holiday feast...pair it with homemade stuffing.

6 boneless, skinless chicken
   breasts
16-oz. can whole berry
   cranberry sauce

8-oz. bottle French salad
   dressing
1½-oz. pkg. onion soup mix

Arrange chicken in an ungreased 13"x9" baking pan; set aside. Combine remaining ingredients; mix well. Pour sauce over chicken breasts; cover with aluminum foil. Bake at 350 degrees for one hour. Serves 6.

Wayne Smith
Wesson, MS

Honey-Pecan Pork Cutlets

To thicken sauce, add a few instant potato flakes. It will be hearty and extra yummy.

1 lb. boneless pork loin cutlets
½ c. all-purpose flour
3 T. butter, divided

¼ c. honey
¼ c. chopped pecans

You won't believe that something so good can be so simple.

Kathy

Pound pork to ¼-inch thickness; coat with flour. Heat one tablespoon butter in a large skillet over medium heat. Add pork and sauté about 5 to 6 minutes or until brown on both sides. In a small bowl, soften remaining butter and mix with honey and pecans; add to skillet. Stir sauce gently. Cover and simmer for 7 to 8 minutes or until juices run clear. Remove to a serving platter, and spoon sauce over pork. Serves 2 to 3.

Kathy Grashoff
Fort Wayne, IN

Savory Cranberry Chicken

Slow-Cooker Ham & Broccoli Meal-in-One

This main dish rice casserole cooks up while you are away...a truly trouble-free meal!

1 c. long-cooking rice, cooked
16-oz. jar pasteurized process
    cheese sauce
2 10¾-oz. cans cream of
    chicken soup

2 16-oz. pkgs. frozen chopped
    broccoli, thawed
salt and pepper to taste
1 lb. cooked ham cubes

Combine all ingredients in a slow cooker except ham. Cover and cook on low setting for 3½ hours. Add ham, and mix well. Cover and cook for an additional 15 to 30 minutes. Serves 6 to 8.

Hope Davenport
Portland, TX

Even my kids enjoy this dish...it's a great way to get them to eat their broccoli.

Hope

herbed garlic butter

Keep a crock of herbed garlic butter in the fridge for jazzing up steamed veggies or making toasty garlic bread. Simply blend a teaspoon each of Italian seasoning, dried mustard and garlic powder into a ½ cup of softened butter. Mmm, good!

Italian Mini Meatloaves

Baked in a muffin tin, these individual meatloaves are a great make-ahead main dish.

1 lb. ground beef
16-oz. pkg. stuffing mix
1 c. water

1 t. Italian seasoning
1 c. tomato-basil pasta sauce
¾ c. shredded mozzarella cheese

Mix together beef, stuffing mix, water and seasoning until well blended. Spray a muffin tin with non-stick vegetable spray. Press mixture evenly into 12 muffin cups. Make a small well in the center of each mini loaf; spoon some sauce into each well. Bake, uncovered, at 375 degrees for about 30 minutes or until cooked through. Sprinkle with cheese, and bake for 5 to 7 minutes more until cheese is melted. Makes 12 mini meatloaves.

Cari Simons
Lawrence, KS

meatloaf mix-ups

Don't toss out the last cheese crackers or taco chips in the package. Crush them and add to meatloaf instead of store-bought stuffing mix or dry bread crumbs. Your thrifty meatloaf will be even more delicious than usual.

Chicken Alfredo Florentine

Hot, creamy chicken pasta is on the table in minutes!

8-oz. pkg. fettucine pasta,
    uncooked
2 T. butter, sliced
17-oz. jar Alfredo pasta sauce

10-oz. pkg. frozen chopped
    spinach, thawed and drained
6-oz. pkg. grilled chicken strips
Garnish: grated Parmesan cheese

Cook pasta according to package directions; drain well and toss with butter. In a large saucepan, combine pasta, sauce, spinach and chicken. Simmer over low heat for about 15 minutes until heated through. Sprinkle with Parmesan cheese, and serve. Serves 4.

Lorrie Smith
Drummonds, TN

I enjoyed a similar dish at a restaurant and decided to see if I could duplicate it at home. This is what I came up with...I think it turned out pretty well.

Lorrie

French Bread-Sausage Pizza

A quick and easy dinner...kids will love to eat this as much as they'll love helping Mom make it! Change it up any way you like, adding other pizza toppings to your own taste.

1 loaf French bread, halved
    lengthwise
15-oz. can pizza sauce
1 lb. ground pork sausage,
    browned and drained

3½-oz. pkg. sliced pepperoni
8-oz. pkg. shredded mozzarella
    cheese

Place both halves of loaf on an ungreased baking sheet, cut side up. Spread with pizza sauce; top with sausage, pepperoni and cheese. Bake at 350 degrees for 15 minutes or until cheese is melted. Slice to serve. Serves 6 to 8.

Christine Gordon
Rapid City, SD

Poppy's Onion Pizza

For a light vegetarian dinner, this pizza is the best choice.

My dad became a wonderful cook when he retired...he passed this traditional Italian recipe on to me.

Lisa

3 T. olive oil, divided
10-inch refrigerated pizza crust
2 onions, diced
garlic powder to taste

paprika to taste
Optional: salt and pepper
   to taste

Lightly coat pizza pan with one tablespoon olive oil; place pizza dough into pan. Coat dough with one tablespoon olive oil; set aside. Sauté onions in remaining olive oil until golden; spread evenly over the pizza dough, lightly pressing down. Sprinkle with garlic powder and paprika; add salt and pepper, if desired. Bake at 425 degrees for 20 minutes or until golden. Serves 8.

Lisa Arning
Garden City, NY

pizza party!

A make-it-yourself pizza party is great for pizza-loving youngsters! It's cheaper than ordering from a pizza shop and doubles as a fun party activity. Set out ready-to-bake pizza crusts and lots of toppings, and let party guests get creative.

Baked Barbecue Chicken

Bacon and mushrooms transform ordinary barbecue chicken.

4 boneless, skinless chicken
   breasts
1 c. all-purpose flour
6 to 7 slices bacon

8-oz. can mushroom pieces,
   drained
1½ c. barbecue sauce

Coat chicken breasts in flour; arrange in an ungreased 13"x9" baking pan. Lay bacon across tops of chicken; bake, uncovered, at 400 degrees for 45 minutes. Drain. Top with mushroom pieces and barbecue sauce. Bake 15 minutes longer. Serves 4.

Heather Riley
Johnston, IA

dinner themes

Set a regular dinner theme for each night, and it'll be a snap to make out your shopping list. Some tasty, budget-friendly themes are Spaghetti Night, Soup & Salad Night, and Leftovers Night...your family is sure to think of other favorites, too.

Tamale Pie

Ready-made tamales make this pie oh-so quick.

2 15-oz. cans beef tamales, divided
15-oz. can chili, divided
9¼-oz. pkg. corn chips, divided
1 onion, minced and divided
2 c. shredded Cheddar cheese, divided

Chop one can of tamales; set aside. Spread one cup chili in the bottom of a greased 2-quart casserole dish; layer half the corn chips, half the onion and chopped tamales on top. Sprinkle with half the cheese; repeat layers, ending with whole tamales topped with cheese. Cover and bake at 350 degrees for one hour. Let cool for 10 minutes before serving. Serves 12.

Kelly Cook
Dunedin, FL

personalized place markers

Hosting a summer get-together? Put together topiary place markers...mount tiny birdhouses on dowels, and then secure in pretty personalized painted pots. You can even send them home as party favors.

Shrimp & Tomato Italiano

A fabulous one-dish meal tossed together in a skillet…it's an easy suppertime winner!

Once when I was staying with my grandmother, we had a heavy snowstorm. I decided to make lunch with the ingredients we had on hand…this yummy dish was the result.

Rebecca

3 14½-oz. cans diced tomatoes
   with Italian herbs
1 T. garlic, minced
1¼ lbs. cooked medium
   shrimp, tails removed

12-oz. pkg. refrigerated fettucine
   pasta, uncooked
salt and pepper to taste

Combine tomatoes with garlic in a deep skillet over medium heat. Add shrimp to skillet; bring to a boil. Add pasta, stirring to prevent sticking. (Do not cook pasta ahead of time, to avoid overcooking.) Boil pasta to desired doneness, 3 to 4 minutes. Remove from heat; toss to mix well. Add salt and pepper to taste. Serves 3 to 4.

Rebecca Richardson
Boscawen, NH

quick thaw

Thaw frozen shrimp quickly by placing the shrimp in a colander and running cold water over it…they'll be ready to cook in minutes.

Glazed Corned Beef

This brisket simmers all day in the slow cooker until fork-tender. Baste it before you serve...so simple!

4 to 5-lb. corned beef brisket
2½ T. mustard
2 t. prepared horseradish

2 T. red wine vinegar
¼ c. honey

In a 5-quart slow cooker, cover brisket with water. Cover and cook on low setting for 10 to 12 hours or until tender. Place corned beef in an ungreased 13"x9" baking pan. In a small bowl, combine mustard, horseradish, vinegar and honey; baste beef. Bake, uncovered, at 400 degrees for 20 minutes or until brisket browns; baste occasionally. Serves 4.

Claire Bertram
Lexington, KY

Stuffed Chicken Breasts

For a simple side, grill some asparagus spears along with the chicken.

4 boneless, skinless chicken
    breasts
8-oz. container garlic & herb
    cream cheese spread

8 slices bacon

Flatten chicken breasts between wax paper. Spread each chicken breast with cream cheese, and roll up. Wrap 2 slices of bacon around each roll; secure with toothpicks. Place on a grill or in a grill pan over medium heat. Cook, turning occasionally for 20 to 25 minutes or until golden and chicken juices run clear. Serves 4.

Ursala Armstrong
Odenville, AL

Zesty Picante Chicken

Spice up suppertime with yummy southwestern-style chicken breasts... made in the slow cooker!

4 boneless, skinless chicken
    breasts
16-oz. jar picante sauce
15½-oz. can black beans, drained
    and rinsed

4 slices American cheese
2¼ c. cooked rice
Optional: green onions

Place chicken in a 5-quart slow cooker; add picante sauce. Spread black beans over the top. Cover and cook on high setting for 3 hours or until juices run clear when chicken is pierced with a fork. Top with cheese slices; cover and heat until melted. Spoon over rice to serve. Garnish with green onions, if desired. Serves 4.

Sonya Collett
Sioux City, IA

We like to double the recipe and just roll up the leftovers in tortillas...tomorrow's dinner is ready.

Sonya

homemade chicken broth

Savory chicken broth...free! After slicing the meat from a deli chicken, cover the bones with water in a stockpot. Onion and celery trimmings can be added, too. Simmer gently for 30 to 40 minutes, then strain and refrigerate liquid in recipe-size containers.

Smoky Hobo Dinner

Away from home all day? This slow-cooker creation will have dinner waiting for you!

5 potatoes, peeled and quartered
1 head cabbage, coarsely chopped
16-oz. pkg. baby carrots
1 onion, thickly sliced
salt and pepper to taste

14-oz. pkg. smoked pork sausage, sliced into 2-inch pieces
½ c. water

Spray a 5- to 6-quart slow cooker with non-stick vegetable spray. Layer vegetables, sprinkling each layer with salt and pepper. Place sausage on top. Pour water down one side of slow cooker. Cover and cook on low setting for 6 to 8 hours. Serves 6.

Julie Pak
Henryetta, OK

help yourself!

Slow-cooker meals make parties so easy...thrifty, too. Cook up some saucy bratwurst or hot dogs, set out bakery-fresh rolls and potato salad, and you're ready to let guests help themselves.

Spicy Chicken Casserole

A hearty, creamy dinner in one dish...with just four ingredients!

It's even speedier to put together if you have leftover cooked chicken on hand.

Martha

4 to 5 boneless, skinless chicken breasts
2 10¾-oz. cans cream of chicken soup

2 10¾-oz. cans nacho cheese soup
3 to 4 c. tortilla chips, crushed and divided

Cover chicken breasts with water in a large saucepan. Simmer over medium-high heat just until cooked through. Drain, saving broth for another use. Cool chicken slightly; shred into bite-size pieces, and set aside. Combine soups in a saucepan. Stir well; cook over medium heat until bubbly. Remove from heat. In a greased 13"x9" baking pan, layer half of chopped chicken, half of soup mixture and half of the crushed chips. Repeat layers. Cover and bake at 350 degrees for 20 minutes or until heated through. Serves 6.

Martha Stephens
Sibley, LA

a clear choice

If you need a new casserole dish, consider getting a deep 13"x9" glass baking dish. It retains heat well to create crisp golden crusts, cleans up easily, and can be used for both savory mains and sweet desserts.

Angie's Pasta & Sauce

Homemade sauce is so simple to prepare. You'll love the taste of both the sauce and the freshly grated Parmesan on top.

6 to 8 roma tomatoes, halved,
    seeded and diced
1 to 2 cloves garlic, minced
½ c. butter, melted
1 T. dried basil

8-oz. pkg. angel hair pasta,
    cooked
Garnish: freshly grated
    Parmesan cheese

Combine tomatoes and garlic in a saucepan. Simmer over medium heat 15 minutes; set aside. Blend together butter and basil; add to pasta. Toss to coat. Stir in tomato mixture, and garnish. Serves 4 to 6.

Angie Whitmore
Farmington, UT

garden party centerpiece

For a garden party, arrange flowers or even vegetable bouquets in produce baskets or miniature watering cans. Insert seed packets attached to bamboo skewers into the arrangements, or use them to identify the dishes you're serving.

Tac-Olé Bubble Bake

This is a scrumptious way to use up leftover taco beef!

I usually fix extra ground beef when I make tacos so I can freeze it and make this casserole the following week.

Tanya

2 12-oz. tubes refrigerated
   biscuits, quartered
½ to 1 lb. ground beef, browned
   and drained, or leftover
   taco beef

1½ c. salsa
1 c. shredded Cheddar cheese
Optional: sour cream, shredded
   lettuce, diced tomatoes

Arrange biscuit quarters in the bottom of a 2-quart casserole dish that has been sprayed with non-stick vegetable spray. Spread beef (or leftover taco beef) evenly over biscuits. Spoon salsa over beef; top with cheese. Cover with aluminum foil, and bake at 350 degrees for 35 to 45 minutes. Garnish as desired. Serves 4 to 6.

Tanya Belt
Newcomerstown, OH

weekly meatless mains

Try serving a meatless main once a week...it's not only economical, it's healthy too. Cheese-filled manicotti with tomato sauce, vegetable stir-fry over rice, or even an irresistible side dish such as hashbrown casserole can stand alone as the main course.

Bacon Florentine Fettuccine

Microwave frozen creamed spinach to create the pasta sauce...a tasty one-dish meal in a snap.

16-oz. pkg. fettuccine, uncooked
2 10-oz. pkgs. frozen creamed
    spinach
½ lb. bacon, crisply cooked and
    chopped
⅛ t. garlic powder
½ c. plus 2 T. grated Parmesan
    cheese, divided
pepper to taste

This is incredibly simple and so fast to prepare.

Barbara

Prepare fettuccine according to package directions; drain, reserving ¾ cup of cooking liquid. Return fettuccine and reserved liquid to the pan. Microwave spinach according to package directions. Add spinach, bacon and garlic powder to saucepan. Transfer spinach mixture to a serving dish, and stir in ½ cup cheese. Season with pepper, and sprinkle with remaining cheese. Serves 4.

Barbara Adamson
Oviedo, FL

State Fair Pork Chops

The sweet and tangy glaze coating these pork chops is lip-smacking good!

2 eggs
¼ c. mustard
¼ c. brown sugar, packed
⅓ c. red wine vinegar
8 pork chops
seasoned salt to taste

First-prize winner!

Heather

In a small bowl, beat together eggs and mustard. In a separate small bowl, dissolve brown sugar in vinegar; add to egg mixture. Brush both sides of pork chops with brown sugar mixture, and place into a greased 13"x9" baking pan. Sprinkle with seasoned salt; grill 10 minutes on each side or until juices run clear when pierced with a fork, basting at least once during grilling time. Serves 6 to 8.

Heather Denk
Naperville, IL

Easy Chicken Dinner

Serve with piping hot biscuits for a complete meal in minutes.

2 10¾-oz. cans cream of
   chicken soup
2 10-oz. cans chicken, drained
15¼-oz. can peas, drained

8-oz. can sliced mushrooms,
   drained
8-oz. pkg. angel hair pasta,
   cooked

Mix soup, chicken, peas and mushrooms together in a saucepan; heat through. Spoon over hot pasta. Serves 6 to 8.

Katrina Pierce
Indianapolis, IN

spaghetti on the side

Make a simple, satisfying side in a flash with a package of thin spaghetti. Toss cooked pasta with a little butter and grated Parmesan cheese, or try chopped tomato and a drizzle of olive oil...that's all it takes!

Cheeseburger Bake

For a neighbor in need or a new mom, duplicate this recipe using a 9"
round disposable foil pan.

A hearty meal in itself!

Jennifer

8-oz. tube refrigerated crescent rolls	1¼-oz. pkg. taco seasoning mix
1 lb. ground beef, browned	15-oz. can tomato sauce
	2 c. shredded Cheddar cheese

Unroll crescent roll dough; press into a greased 9" round baking
pan, pinching seams closed. Bake, uncovered, at 350 degrees for 10
minutes; set aside. Add beef, seasoning and tomato sauce to a 12" skillet; heat through, about 7 minutes. Pour into crust; sprinkle cheese on
top. Bake, uncovered, for 10 to 15 minutes. Let stand 5 minutes before
serving. Serves 4.

Jennifer Dutcher
Lewis Center, OH

Easy Slow-Cooker Steak

Like lots of gravy? Use two envelopes of soup mix and two cans of soup.

2 to 2½ lb. round steak	10¾-oz. can cream of
1½-oz. pkg. onion soup mix	mushroom soup

Slice steak into 5 serving-size pieces; place in a slow cooker. Add
soup mix, ¼ cup water and soup. Cover and cook on low setting for
6 to 8 hours. Makes 5 servings.

Ashley Whitehead
Sidney, TX

Cheeseburger Bake

Marshmallow
Fruit Dip, page 238

quick-fix snacks

Put an end to movie-night munchies and after-school appetites.

Snack solutions are at your fingertips! Offer *Pepperoni Pizza*

Bites (page 240) or *Apple Wheels (page 257)* when

the kids get off the bus or at the next

sleepover. Serve up a bowl of

Honey-Glazed Snack Mix

(page 246) or *Cinnamon-*

Sugar Crisp Strips

(page 248), and

you'll satisfy a

whole crowd.

Marshmallow Fruit Dip

(pictured on page 236)

Try this creamy dip with cinnamon graham crackers or on a slice of pound cake...yum!

The kids forget fruit is good for them once they start dippin' away.

Susan

8-oz. pkg. cream cheese, softened   7-oz. jar marshmallow creme
3 T. thawed frozen orange juice
      concentrate

Blend cream cheese and orange juice concentrate together until smooth; stir in marshmallow creme. Refrigerate until well chilled. Makes about 2 cups.

Susan Young
Madison, AL

chill out!

Keep fruit dip chilled in a vintage pie plate filled with crushed ice. Nestle a small bowl into the ice to chill the dip...country style!

Chocolate-Covered Peanuts

Last-minute dinner invitation? Whip up these yummy clusters, and pack into a vintage tin for the hosts.

1 c. semi-sweet chocolate chips   1 T. water
¼ c. corn syrup   2 c. salted peanuts

    Combine chocolate, corn syrup and water in a double boiler; stir until melted. Remove from heat, and stir in peanuts until well coated. Drop mixture by teaspoonfuls onto baking sheets lined with wax paper. Cover baking sheets with aluminum foil, and chill until firm. Makes 3 dozen.

yogurt & cereal parfaits

Save bottom-of-the-box leftovers of crunchy breakfast cereal in a canister. Layer the crumbs with sweet fruit yogurt in parfait glasses to create a quick, healthful treat.

Pepperoni Pizza Bites

Get creative and try this recipe with alternative toppings...you'll have a blast!

So fun to make
with the kids.

Nancy

11-oz. tube refrigerated thin
    pizza crust
½ c. pizza sauce

8 slices pepperoni
½ c. shredded mozzarella cheese

    Do not unroll pizza crust; cut into 8 equal pieces. Arrange dough 3 inches apart on parchment-lined baking sheet. Flatten each piece of dough into a 2½" circle. Spoon pizza sauce into each center. Top each pizza with pepperoni and cheese. Bake at 400 degrees for 12 minutes or until golden and cheese melts. Makes 8 pizzas.

Nancy Kremkus
Ann Arbor, MI

veggie pizza

Gardens turn up the best pizza toppers...try something new like chopped spinach, green onions, chives, cilantro, asparagus, sliced roma tomatoes or even shredded carrots.

Chinese Chicken Wings

This recipe can also be made with chicken drummies. Serve them with ranch dressing for dipping and celery stalks for a cool crunch.

½ c. soy sauce
½ c. brown sugar, packed
½ c. butter

¼ c. water
½ t. dry mustard
4 lbs. chicken wings

Combine all ingredients except wings in a saucepan; cook for 5 minutes over medium heat. Place wings on an ungreased large shallow baking pan; brush with sauce. Bake at 350 degrees for one hour, turning occasionally and brushing with remaining sauce. Makes about 20 wings.

Trisha Donley
Pinedale, WY

This is a very easy recipe, a quick go-to that's so yummy.

Trisha

candle creations

A vintage enamelware cup easily becomes a whimsical candle for picnics on the porch. Use melted beeswax and a wick…craft stores sell all the supplies and instructions you'll need. Remember to place candles on a safe surface for burning, and never leave them unattended.

Caramel Apple Dip

A quick and easy dip…perfect for autumn gatherings.

8-oz. pkg. cream cheese, softened
¼ c. honey
½ c. caramel ice cream topping
¼ t. cinnamon
3 to 4 green apples, cored and
   sliced

In a medium serving bowl, combine cream cheese, honey, caramel topping and cinnamon; beat until smooth. Chill in refrigerator. Serve with apple slices. Makes 2 cups.

Brenda Harrell
Beulaville, NC

tea lights afloat

Need a pretty centerpiece? Float tea lights in glass dessert dishes. Group three or four dishes per table, and light for a magical night.

Sweet Potato Chips

Spicy and oh-so tasty!

1 t. sugar
1 t. salt
1½ T. chili powder

¼ to ½ t. cumin
2 sweet potatoes, thinly sliced

Combine sugar, salt, chili powder and cumin in a small mixing bowl; set aside. Place potato slices on a lightly greased baking sheet. Sprinkle with half of sugar mixture. Bake at 325 degrees for 15 minutes; turn slices over, and sprinkle with remaining sugar mixture. Bake an additional 15 minutes. Remove from oven, and place on wire rack to cool. Serves 4.

Lisa Donnelly
Oak Lawn, IL

Chip Dip

Pick up a bag of baked potato chips to serve with this delectable dip.

8-oz. pkg. cream cheese, softened
2 T. milk
⅓ c. catsup

2 T. onion, chopped
2 T. French salad dressing

In a large bowl, combine all ingredients with an electric mixer. Refrigerate for 2 to 3 hours before serving. Serves 10 to 12.

Sheila Vukovich
North Canton, OH

Honey-Glazed Snack Mix

Pack in plastic bags for school day snacks, or pour in a bowl for a movie night treat.

This recipe is from my friend, Mary Beth Mitchell. I like the taste of this best when I use fresh honey from the farmers' market or orchard.

Cindy

5 c. corn and rice cereal
3 c. mini pretzel twists
2 c. pecan halves

½ c. honey
½ c. butter, melted

Combine cereal, pretzels and pecans in a large bowl; set aside. Blend together honey and margarine. Pour over cereal mixture; toss to coat. Spread on ungreased baking sheets. Bake at 300 degrees for 10 minutes. Stir and continue to bake an additional 10 to 15 minutes. Pour onto wax paper, and cool completely. Store in airtight containers. Makes about 10 cups.

Cindy Elliott
Modesto, IL

summertime scrapbook

Put everyone's favorite summertime photos together in a scrapbook to be enjoyed year-round! Add postcards from family trips, ticket stubs from the county fair, and other mementos, too.

Cinnamon-Sugar Crisp Strips

Once you taste these, you'll have trouble walking away from more. Try dipping them in warm cinnamon-apple pie filling.

When my mother taught me to make this recipe, we used wonton wrappers. I modified it slightly and now use flour tortillas, but both taste great.

Melissa

1 T. cinnamon
1 c. sugar
oil for deep frying

8 10-inch flour tortillas, cut into 1-inch strips

Combine cinnamon and sugar in a bowl; set aside. Heat 2 inches of oil in a heavy skillet over medium-high heat. Add 5 to 7 tortilla strips at a time; cook for 20 to 40 seconds on each side until crisp. Drain on a paper towel-lined plate for 5 minutes, then sprinkle with cinnamon-sugar mixture. Place strips and remaining cinnamon-sugar mixture into a paper bag. Gently toss tortilla strips to coat well. Remove from bag, and arrange on a serving plate. Serves 6 to 8.

Melissa Fraser
Valencia, CA

apple pie filling

When apples are in season, bring home a bushel and make apple pie filling to store in your freezer! Prepare a favorite recipe, then let the pie filling cool for 30 minutes. Spoon it into freezer containers, leaving ½-inch headspace. Let cool about an hour, seal containers, and freeze for up to one year.

Seasoned Oyster Crackers

So good by themselves or sprinkled into homemade soups and stews.

1½ c. oil
2 1-oz. pkgs. ranch salad
    dressing mix

1 T. lemon pepper
1 T. dill weed
2 10-oz. pkgs. oyster crackers

    Whisk first 4 ingredients together; pour over oyster crackers. Toss gently; spread on an ungreased baking sheet. Bake at 225 degrees for one hour, stirring every 15 minutes. Makes 24 servings.

Jen Sell
Farmington, MN

Nanny's Stuffed Celery

A crunchy and savory snack to satisfy your munchies!

This recipe is a family tradition started by my grandmother in the 1940s. She always brought it to our holiday dinners.

Dawn

1½ c. chopped walnuts
1 c. green olives, chopped and
    2 T. juice reserved
2 8-oz. pkgs. cream cheese,
    softened

¼ c. milk
2 bunches celery, cut into 2-inch
    pieces

    In a small bowl, combine walnuts and olives. In a large bowl, blend cream cheese and walnut mixture; add milk and reserved olive juice. Mix thoroughly with a fork. Stuff each celery piece with filling. Let chill one hour before serving. Makes 4 dozen.

Dawn Mills
Falls Church, VA

Italian Bagel Chips

A flavorful crunch from a baked chip...also a great side with sandwiches.

9 frozen mini bagels, thawed
   and split
1½ t. Italian seasoning

¼ t. onion powder
¼ t. garlic powder
salt and pepper to taste

Cut each bagel half crosswise into 4 slices. Place slices in a single layer on an ungreased baking sheet; lightly coat tops with non-stick vegetable spray. In a small bowl, combine remaining ingredients; sprinkle evenly over bagels. Bake at 375 degrees for 12 minutes or until crisp. Makes 3 dozen chips.

bagel chip dip

Blend together a package of ranch salad dressing mix and cream cheese...serve with Italian bagel chips for a delightful surprise.

Bacon Quesadillas

These savory snacks have zing...what flavor!

1 c. shredded Colby Jack cheese
¼ c. bacon bits
¼ c. green onion, thinly sliced
Optional: 4½-oz. can green chiles

Optional: ¼ c. red or green
    pepper, chopped
4 6-inch flour tortillas
Garnish: sour cream, salsa

Combine cheese, bacon bits and onion in a small bowl; add chiles and peppers, if desired. Sprinkle mixture equally over one half of each tortilla. Fold tortillas in half; press lightly to seal edges. Arrange on a lightly greased baking sheet. Bake at 400 degrees for 8 to 10 minutes until edges are lightly golden. Top with a dollop of sour cream and salsa. Serves 4.

Edward Kielar
Perrysburg, OH

after-school treats

Need a quick after-school snack to tide the kids over until suppertime? Hand out little bags of crunchy treats...just toss together bite-size cereal squares, raisins or dried cranberries and a few chocolate-covered candies.

Rocky Mountain Cereal Bars

These homemade snack bars will disappear quickly!

⅔ c. sugar
⅔ c. corn syrup
1 c. creamy peanut butter
6 c. doughnut-shaped multi-grain
    oat cereal

¾ to 1 c. sweetened dried
    cranberries

Combine sugar, corn syrup and peanut butter in a large saucepan over low heat. Stirring mixture constantly, heat through until peanut butter is melted. Remove from heat. Add cereal and dried cranberries; mix well. Spread cereal mixture evenly into a lightly greased 13"x9" baking pan. Cool completely; cut into bars. Makes about 2½ dozen bars.

Karen Ensign
Providence, UT

Our whole family loves these bars, whether as a snack, dessert, or even breakfast.

Karen

sticky fingers

Before pressing bars into a baking dish, run fingers under cold water. This will keep the treats from sticking to your hands.

Cricket Crunchies

Don't let the name fool you...cinnamon-sugar pecans are irresistible!

1 egg white
2 c. chopped pecans

¼ c. sugar
1 T. cinnamon

In a medium bowl, combine egg white and pecans together until coated and sticky. In a small bowl, combine sugar and cinnamon; sprinkle over pecans, stirring until evenly coated. Spread pecans on an ungreased baking sheet. Bake at 350 degrees for 30 minutes; remove from oven, and cool for 5 minutes. Break apart, and store in an airtight container. Makes 2 cups.

Cricket Hansen
West Jordan, UT

Crispy Treats

Pair these treats with a glass of milk...it'll hit the spot.

5 c. crispy rice cereal
40 marshmallows

½ t. cinnamon
1 c. chopped walnuts

Mix together all ingredients in a large saucepan over low heat. Pour mixture into a greased 13"x9" baking pan. Refrigerate until set; cut into squares. Serves 16 to 18.

Lori Marcar
San Jose, CA

Apple Wheels

Your kids can help you pack the apples with the yummy filling...but they may have a hard time waiting for them to chill.

¼ c. creamy peanut butter

2 t. honey

½ c. semi-sweet mini chocolate
    chips

1 T. raisins

4 red or yellow apples, cored

Combine peanut butter and honey in a bowl; stir in chocolate chips and raisins. Fill centers of apples with peanut butter mixture; refrigerate for one hour. Slice apples into ¼-inch rings to serve. Serves 4.

Jackie Smulski
Lyons, IL

a yummy change

Peanut butter is a favorite with kids big and little. When making your next snack or sandwich, try cashew or almond butter.

Caramel-Marshmallow Delights

Sweet and chewy...a winning combination.

14-oz. can sweetened condensed
   milk
½ c. butter

14-oz. pkg. caramels, unwrapped
16-oz. pkg. marshmallows
10-oz. pkg. crispy rice cereal

Combine milk, butter and caramels in a heavy saucepan over medium heat; stir until butter and caramels melt and mixture is smooth. Remove from heat; quickly dip marshmallows into mixture, and then roll in rice cereal. Arrange on an aluminum foil-lined baking sheet; refrigerate for 30 minutes. Remove from baking sheet; refrigerate in an airtight container. Makes 5 to 6 dozen.

Shelley Haverkate
Grandville, MI

homemade popsicles

Need a quick snack for the kids? Make fruit pops! Blend together fresh or canned fruit with fruit juice, and pour into ice cube trays or small paper cups. Insert wooden sticks before freezing.

Chocolate Chip Tea
Cookies, page 301

delectable desserts

Sometimes the best-tasting sweets are made with the fewest ingredients. Your party guests will rave about Chocolate-Marshmallow Pie (page 269) or Pineapple-Cherry Cake (page 272). Save time by making Cake Mix Brownies (page 290) or Banana Bread Trifle (page 293). Here you'll find page after page of melt-in-your-mouth desserts.

Cherry Dream Pie

Perfect for picnics and potlucks.

8-oz. pkg. cream cheese, softened
½ c. powdered sugar
8-oz. container frozen whipped
    topping, thawed

9-inch graham cracker pie crust
14½-oz. can cherry pie filling

Blend cream cheese and powdered sugar together until smooth and creamy; fold in whipped topping. Spread into pie crust forming a well in the center; fill with pie filling. Chill until firm before serving. Serves 8.

Clara Buckman
Waverly, KY

a cheery bouquet

Snip new branches from a pussy willow and pair up with the very first forsythia blooms for a cheery spring bouquet…instead of a vase, gather the stems in a nostalgic pitcher!

Easiest-Ever Cheesecake

Easiest-Ever Cheesecake

You can also drizzle melted chocolate on top for a rich and flavorful twist.

12-oz. pkg. vanilla wafers,
    crushed
1 c. plus 2 T. sugar, divided
½ c. butter, melted
2 8-oz. pkgs. cream cheese,
    softened

12-oz. container frozen whipped
    topping, thawed
Optional: fresh raspberries

    Combine vanilla wafers, 2 tablespoons sugar and butter; press into the bottom of a 13"x9" baking pan. In a separate bowl, blend together remaining sugar and cream cheese; fold in whipped topping. Spread over wafer crust; chill until firm. Garnish with fresh raspberries, if desired. Serves 12 to 15.

Linda Lewanski
Cosby, TN

Butter Pecan-Peach Cake

So refreshing in the summer, or serve warm on chilly days…a yummy treat either way!

29-oz. can sliced peaches
18¼-oz. pkg. butter pecan or
    yellow cake mix

½ c. butter, melted
1 c. chopped pecans
1 c. sweetened flaked coconut

    Pour peaches and syrup in the bottom of an ungreased 13"x9" baking pan. Cover with dry cake mix; drizzle butter over the top. Sprinkle with pecans and coconut. Bake, uncovered, at 350 degrees for 30 to 35 minutes. Serves 18 to 24.

Carole Akers
Bellevue, OH

Open-Face Peach Pie

Bring this to the next summer backyard party, and you'll be popular!

This favorite pie recipe was handed down to me from my grandmother.

Christy

1 c. sugar
2 T. cornstarch
9-inch pie crust

6 peaches, peeled, pitted and
    halved
1 c. whipping cream

Mix together sugar and cornstarch; spread ¾ of mixture into pie crust. Arrange peaches on top; sprinkle with remaining sugar mixture. Pour cream evenly over peaches; bake at 400 degrees for 10 minutes. Reduce heat to 350 degrees; bake an additional 40 minutes. Serves 8.

Christy Hughes
Provo, UT

get to the core

An easy way to core apples and peaches…slice fruit in half, and then use a melon baller to scoop out the core.

Creamy Pineapple Dessert

Super sweet and fruity.

My sister, Lori, shared this recipe with me... it came with the funny but descriptive name, "Four Tins and a Tub!"

Lisa

20-oz. can crushed pineapple, drained
20-oz. can pineapple chunks, drained
14-oz. can sweetened condensed milk

22-oz. can lemon pie filling
8-oz. container frozen whipped topping, thawed

Mix all ingredients in a large bowl. Keep chilled until serving time. Serve cold. Serves 8 to 10.

Lisa Johnson
Hallsville, TX

Orange Cloud Dessert

Here's a refreshing citrus dessert for those hot summer nights.

2 c. water
3-oz. pkg. orange gelatin mix
3.4-oz. pkg. instant vanilla pudding mix

8-oz. container frozen whipped topping, thawed
11-oz. can mandarin oranges, drained

In a medium saucepan, bring water to a boil over medium heat. Add gelatin and pudding mixes; whisk and boil for 2 minutes. Chill in saucepan just until set; stir in whipped topping and oranges. Transfer to a serving bowl; chill until ready to serve. Serves 8.

Julie Brown
Malvern, OH

Chocolate-Marshmallow Pie

(pictured on page 2)

A pretty presentation and tasty too!

16 marshmallows
5 1.45-oz. milk chocolate candy
    bars with almonds, divided
½ c. milk
8-oz. container whipping cream
9-inch graham cracker pie crust

Heat marshmallows, 4 candy bars and milk in a double boiler until marshmallows and chocolate melt; stir often. Remove from heat; stir in whipping cream. Pour into pie crust; refrigerate until firm. Use a vegetable peeler to make chocolate curls with the remaining candy bar. Garnish with chocolate curls. Serves 8.

Brenda Neal
Taneyville, MO

I received this recipe from a dear friend who's 90 years old... we make this decadent dessert often and enjoy it every time.

Brenda

Raspberry Cream Pie

Use blackberries instead of raspberries for a sweet change.

14-oz. can sweetened condensed
    milk
⅔ c. frozen raspberry-lemonade
    concentrate, thawed
8-oz. container frozen whipped
    topping, thawed
1 c. frozen raspberries, divided
9-inch graham cracker pie crust

In a large mixing bowl, combine milk and concentrate; mix well. Blend in whipped topping. Spoon ½ cup raspberries into the bottom of pie crust; top with filling, and chill for 6 hours. Top with remaining raspberries before serving. Serves 8.

Jennifer Barga
Dublin, OH

Berry Crumble

Instant oatmeal is the key to the scrumptious topping.

4 c. blackberries or blueberries
1 to 2 T. sugar
3 T. butter, softened

3 1½-oz. pkgs. quick-cooking oats with maple and brown sugar

Toss berries and sugar together in an ungreased 9" pie plate; set aside. Cut butter into quick-cooking oats until coarse crumbs form; sprinkle over berries. Bake at 375 degrees until topping is golden, about 30 to 35 minutes. Serves 6.

Sandy Bernards
Valencia, CA

brown sugar fix

If a plastic bag of brown sugar has hardened, try this: Add a dampened paper towel to the bag, close it, and microwave for 20 seconds. Press out the lumps with your fingers. If that doesn't do the trick, microwave for another 10 seconds.

Pineapple-Cherry Cake

Serve with either whipped topping or ice cream.

20-oz. can crushed pineapple
18¼-oz. pkg. yellow cake mix,
    divided
15½-oz. can pitted cherries,
    drained

1 c. chopped walnuts or pecans
1 c. butter, melted
Optional: whipped topping

    Evenly spoon pineapple into an ungreased 13"x9" baking pan. Sprinkle half the cake mix on top; spread cherries over cake mix. Sprinkle remaining cake mix over cherries; add nuts. Drizzle with butter; bake at 350 degrees for 45 to 50 minutes. Garnish with whipped topping, if desired. Serves 15.

David Flory
Columbus, OH

Grandmother's Pound Cake

Grandmother's Pound Cake

Try this old-fashioned favorite with sliced strawberries on top.

1 c. butter, softened
1⅔ c. sugar
5 eggs

½ t. vanilla extract
2 c. all-purpose flour

Beat butter until creamy. Blend in sugar, eggs and vanilla. Gradually mix in flour; pour into a greased and floured 9"x5" loaf pan. Bake at 300 degrees for one to 1½ hours. Serves 8 to 10.

Teri Naquin
Melville, LA

Butterscotch Sauce

Dress up slices of store-bought cake or scoops of ice cream with a dollop of this tempting homemade sauce.

½ c. brown sugar, packed
½ c. whipping cream

2 T. butter, sliced

Combine ingredients in a small heavy saucepan. Cook over medium heat, stirring occasionally, until brown sugar dissolves and sauce thickens, about 5 minutes. Cool slightly before serving. Keep refrigerated. Makes ¾ cup.

Vickie
Gooseberry Patch

Busy Day Lemon Cheesecake

Tart, sweet…a special treat!

8-oz. pkg. cream cheese,
   softened
2 c. milk, divided

3½ oz. pkg. instant lemon
   pudding mix
9-inch graham cracker pie crust

In a large bowl, stir cream cheese with a fork until creamy. Add
½ cup milk, a small amount at a time, blending until mixture is very
smooth. Add remaining milk and pudding mix. Beat with whisk for
about one minute or until well mixed; pour into pie crust. Chill for one
hour. Serves 8.

Brenda Erwin
Hurricane, WV

Grasshopper Pie

Taste the refreshing combination of chocolate and mint! Chill the beaters and mixing bowl to speed up the whipping time for cream.

24 chocolate sandwich cookies,
    crushed and divided
¼ c. butter, melted

¼ c. crème de menthe liqueur
7½-oz. jar marshmallow creme
2 c. whipping cream, whipped

In a medium bowl, combine ¾ of cookie crumbs and butter; press into a greased 9" springform pan. In a medium bowl, gradually add crème de menthe to marshmallow creme, mixing until well blended. Blend in whipping cream; pour into pan. Sprinkle with remaining cookie crumbs, and freeze for 2 to 3 hours. Serves 8.

Caryn Dubelko
Dayton, OH

If you don't want to use liqueur, add one to 2 teaspoons mint extract and a couple drops of green food coloring.

Caryn

Old-Fashioned Sugar Cream Pie

Such a simple but delicious pie...just like grandmother used to make it.

2¼ T. all-purpose flour
½ c. sugar
½ c. brown sugar, packed

9-inch pie crust, unbaked
1½ c. milk

Stir together flour and sugars; spoon evenly into pie crust. Pour milk over all. Bake at 450 degrees for 10 minutes; reduce heat to 350 degrees, and bake an additional 35 minutes. Serves 8.

Donna Zink
Lapeer, MI

Mince-Ice Cream Pie

A new taste for mincemeat pie lovers...this is cool and creamy!

1½ qts. French vanilla ice cream, softened
1½ c. mincemeat pie filling
½ c. plus 2 T. chopped walnuts or pecans, divided

9-inch graham cracker pie crust
Optional: frozen whipped topping, thawed

In a large bowl, combine ice cream, mincemeat and ½ cup chopped nuts; mix well. Spread evenly in graham cracker pie crust; freeze pie until firm, 2 to 3 hours. Before serving, spoon whipped cream over pie, if desired. Garnish with remaining nuts. Serves 8.

Jacque Thompson
Clarkston, WA

blueberry topping

For a quick summertime treat, combine blueberries and an equal amount of sugar in a saucepan over low heat until thickened. Let cool, and pour over softened vanilla ice cream.

Ruby's Bavarian Cloud

Experiment with different gelatin flavors to make this recipe your own.

3-oz. pkg. favorite flavored
  gelatin mix
¼ c. sugar
1 c. boiling water
¾ c. chilled fruit juice or cold
  water
½ c. milk

½ t. vanilla extract
16-oz. container frozen whipped
  topping, thawed
Optional: crushed graham
  crackers, chopped fruit,
  whipped topping

In a large bowl, combine gelatin mix, sugar and boiling water. Stir until gelatin is dissolved. Blend in chilled fruit juice or cold water, milk and vanilla; blend in whipped topping. Top with crushed crackers, chopped fruit and whipped topping, if desired. Cover and chill for 4 hours before serving. Serves 6.

Linda Kiffin
Tracy, CA

When I was growing up, Mom would make this fluffy fruit-flavored dessert for me...it was my favorite! After my mom's passing, I was going through her cookbooks and was so excited to find the original recipe, neatly written by her. It brings back many fond memories of Mom.

Linda

whipped cream extras

It's easy to save extra whipped cream. Dollop heaping tablespoonfuls onto a chilled baking sheet, and freeze. Remove from the baking sheet, and store in a plastic zipping bag. To use, place dollops on dessert servings, and let stand a few minutes.

Friendship Peppermint Mud Pie

Minty chocolate ice cream cake with hot fudge topping...oh my!

14-oz. pkg. chocolate sandwich
    cookies, crushed and divided
6 T. butter, melted
½ gal. peppermint ice cream

16-oz. jar hot fudge ice cream
    topping
8-oz. container frozen whipped
    topping, thawed

Set aside ¼ cup cookie crumbs. Combine remaining cookie crumbs and melted butter in a large bowl. Toss to coat. Transfer to a greased 13"x9" baking pan; press crumbs firmly to cover bottom of pan. Spread ice cream over crumb crust. Top with fudge topping. Freeze until firm. At serving time, spread whipped topping to edges. Garnish with reserved cookie crumbs. Serves 12.

Lori Vincent
Alpine, UT

Each Christmas, I get together with four dear friends for brunch. It's great for us to have "girl time." We traditionally eat pie, so whenever I make this recipe, I always think of my best friends!

Lori

spray it instead

Non-stick vegetable spray usually can be used instead of shortening to prepare baking sheets and baking dishes.

Super-Rich Cake

This recipe is a twist on regular German chocolate cake...you'll love it!

18¼-oz. pkg. German chocolate
    cake mix
14-oz. can sweetened condensed
    milk
17-oz. jar butterscotch-caramel
    ice cream topping

8-oz. container frozen whipped
    topping, thawed
6-oz. bar chocolate covered
    toffee candy, crushed

Prepare and bake cake mix in a greased 13"x9" pan according to package directions. Let cool for 10 minutes, then make holes in cake with wooden spoon handle. Pour condensed milk over top; cover with ice cream topping. When completely cooled, frost cake with whipped topping, and sprinkle with candy bar pieces. Refrigerate until ready to serve. Serves 18 to 24.

Crystal Cull
Montgomery, IL

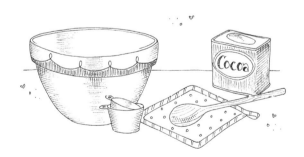

white rings no more

When a chocolate cake recipe calls for the pan to be greased and floured, use cocoa instead of flour. The cocoa will keep a white ring from forming around the outside of the cake.

Hot Fudge-Ice Cream Cake

A delectable make-ahead dessert that takes only minutes to assemble.

16 ice cream sandwiches
16-oz. container frozen whipped
    topping, thawed

2 12-oz. jars hot fudge topping
½ c. Spanish peanuts

Arrange 8 ice cream sandwiches in a single layer in a 13"x9" baking pan. Spread with one-half of whipped topping; add one-third of fudge topping and one-half of nuts. Layer with remaining sandwiches, remaining whipped topping, one-third of fudge topping and remaining peanuts; drizzle with remaining fudge topping. Freeze until firm, about 3 hours. Cut into squares to serve. Serves 16.

Linda Nowak
Cheektowaga, NY

Peach & Blueberry Cobbler

If you want to double the recipe, use a 13"x9" baking pan, and bake for 30 to 40 minutes.

15-oz. can sliced peaches, drained
17.8-oz. pkg. blueberry quick
    bread mix with canned
    blueberries

cinnamon to taste
½ c. butter, melted
Garnish: vanilla ice cream

My friends are always impressed when I serve this dessert...there are never any leftovers!

Amanda

Spread peaches in the bottom of an ungreased 8"x8" baking pan. Drain blueberries, and spread over peaches; sprinkle with cinnamon. Add quick bread mix to melted butter; stir together. Allow mixture to cool slightly; crumble evenly over blueberries. Sprinkle with cinnamon. Bake at 350 degrees for 20 to 30 minutes or until golden. Serve warm with ice cream. Serves 4.

Amanda Clark
Bristol, TN

Graham Cracker Deluxe

This creamy pudding dessert needs to chill for several hours or overnight. You can also assemble it into individual parfait glasses.

Our family has been taking this dessert to our gatherings for years. It never lasts long around my house! It's best made the day before.

Brenda

2 3.4-oz. pkgs. French vanilla
    instant pudding mix
2¾ c. milk
16-oz. container frozen whipped
    topping, thawed

1½ pkgs. sleeves graham
    crackers, divided

Stir together pudding mixes and milk for 2 minutes until mixture is thickened. Blend in whipped topping, and set aside. Line a 13"x9" baking pan with a single layer of graham crackers. Spoon half of pudding mixture over crackers; smooth with the back of a spoon. Add another layer of crackers and remaining pudding mixture; smooth again. Crush any remaining crackers, and sprinkle over top. Cover and refrigerate for several hours to overnight before serving. Serves 12.

Brenda Austin
Durand, MI

coloring sugar

If you need just a little colored sugar for cookies and cupcakes, make it yourself. Just place ¼ cup sugar in a small jar, add a drop or two of food coloring, cover the jar, and shake to blend well. Spread the sugar on wax paper, and let dry.

Peanut Butter Bars

Peanut Butter Bars

With rich butterscotch frosting, these are no ordinary peanut butter bars...wow!

1½ c. graham cracker crumbs
1 c. butter, melted
16-oz. pkg. powdered sugar

1 c. peanut butter
12-oz. pkg. butterscotch chips

Combine first 4 ingredients together; mix well. Press into the bottom of a 13"x9" baking pan; set aside. Melt butterscotch chips in a double boiler; spread over crumb mixture. Refrigerate; cut into bars when cooled. Makes 24 bars.

Angela Sims
Willow Springs, IL

Angel Bars

A sweet, old-fashioned treat made with just four ingredients.

16-oz. pkg. angel food cake mix
22-oz. can lemon pie filling
1 c. sweetened flaked coconut or
    chopped walnuts

Garnish: powdered sugar

In a large bowl, mix together all ingredients except powdered sugar. Spread in a 13"x9" baking pan that has been greased on the bottom only. Bake at 350 degrees for 25 to 30 minutes. Sift powdered sugar over top while still warm; cut into squares. Makes 16 bars.

Paula Spadaccini
Shelburne, VT

Cake Mix Brownies

A scrumptious and inexpensive dessert.

My sweet sister-in-law gave me this recipe more than 30 years ago. Sometimes I top the brownies with chocolate frosting and chopped walnuts.

Kathy

18½-oz. pkg. devil's food
    cake mix
1 egg, beaten
⅓ c. oil

⅓ c. water
Garnish: chocolate frosting,
    chopped walnuts

Stir together all ingredients to make a thick batter. Spread in a greased 13"x9" baking pan. Bake at 350 degrees for 20 to 25 minutes. Cool; cut into squares. Ice squares with frosting and sprinkle with walnuts. Makes one dozen brownies.

Kathy Grashoff
Fort Wayne, IN

cupcake fun!

Cupcakes for dessert tonight? Frost them quickly by dipping in frosting, then toss on some chocolate chips or colored sprinkles just for fun.

Quick Chocolate Mousse

If you're a coffee lover, stir in some instant coffee granules for a yummy mocha mousse.

14-oz. can sweetened condensed
   milk
1 c. cold water
3.9-oz. pkg. instant chocolate
   pudding mix

8-oz. container frozen whipped
   topping, thawed and divided

Whisk together condensed milk and water in a large bowl. Add pudding mix; beat well. Chill 5 minutes. Fold in 2 cups whipped topping; chill until serving time. Garnish with dollops of remaining topping. Serves 8 to 10.

Geneva Rogers
Gillette, WY

Harvest Pumpkin Mousse

Sprinkle with a crunchy topping of crushed gingersnap cookies.

1-oz. pkg. sugar-free instant
   butterscotch pudding mix
1½ c. milk
½ c. canned pumpkin

1 t. pumpkin pie spice
1 c. frozen whipped topping,
   thawed and divided

Whisk together pudding mix and milk for 2 minutes; let stand for 2 minutes until softly set. Blend in pumpkin, spice and ½ cup whipped topping. Spoon into 4 dessert bowls; chill until serving time. Dollop with remaining whipped topping. Serves 4.

Annette Ingram
Grand Rapids, MI

Berry Peachy Twists

Like peach dumplings...these would be a good treat for breakfast, too.

8-oz. tube refrigerated crescent
    rolls
2 T. butter, melted

3-oz. pkg. strawberry gelatin mix
15-oz. can sliced peaches,
    drained and cubed

Separate rolls into 8 triangles. Brush triangles with melted butter; sprinkle with gelatin mix, and top evenly with peaches. Roll up each triangle into a crescent as directed on package. Arrange twists on a greased baking sheet. Bake at 350 degrees for 12 to 15 minutes or until golden. Let cool slightly before serving. Makes 8.

Cyndy Wilber
Ravena, NY

I've been making this treat for our family for almost 40 years. It is quick and easy...even the fussiest kids love it when you let them help!
Cyndy

Banana Bread Trifle

A loaf of banana bread becomes an impressive dessert to feed a crowd... so easy!

1 loaf banana bread, cubed
5¼-oz. pkg. instant vanilla
    pudding mix, prepared
2 to 3 bananas, sliced

12-oz. container frozen whipped
    topping, thawed
Garnish: whipped topping and
    chopped nuts

In a trifle bowl, layer half of bread, pudding, bananas and whipped topping; repeat to fill bowl. Top with whipped topping, and sprinkle nuts over all; refrigerate until ready to serve. Serves 10 to 12.

Joanna Gibson
Fort Polk, LA

Mexican Tea Cookies

Dusted in powdered sugar...these cookies are heavenly.

1 c. butter, softened
¼ c. powdered sugar
2 t. vanilla extract
1 T. water

2 c. all-purpose flour
1 c. chopped pecans
Garnish: powdered sugar

With an electric mixer on medium speed, blend together butter and powdered sugar; add vanilla, water and flour. Stir in pecans. Shape dough in 1" balls. Arrange on an ungreased baking sheet. Bake at 300 degrees for 20 minutes. Remove from oven. When cool, roll in powdered sugar. Makes about 40 cookies.

Kimberly Pfleiderer
Galion, OH

It just wouldn't be Christmas without these cookies.

Kimberly

cookies in a snap

Enjoy fresh-baked cookies at a moment's notice. Roll your favorite cookie dough into balls, and freeze them on a tray, then pop them into a freezer bag. Later, just pull out the number of cookies you need, thaw briefly, and bake.

Crunchy Biscotti

Afternoon or after dinner, you'll crave these treats with your next cup of coffee.

3⅓ c. all-purpose flour
2½ t. baking powder
½ t. salt
¼ c. oil
1¼ c. sugar

2 eggs, beaten
2 egg whites, beaten
Optional: melted white
    chocolate

I like to dress up these cookies with a drizzle of white chocolate!

Jo Ann

Mix flour, baking powder and salt in a large bowl. In a separate bowl, whisk together remaining ingredients. Blend flour mixture into egg mixture. Divide dough into 3 portions; knead each portion 5 to 6 times, and shape into a ball. Place dough balls on a parchment paper-lined 17"x11" baking sheet. Shape into 9-inch logs; flatten slightly. Bake at 375 degrees for 25 minutes. Remove from oven; place logs on a cutting board. Using a serrated bread knife, cut ½-inch thick slices on a slight diagonal. Return slices to baking sheet, cut-side up. Bake for an additional 10 minutes at 375 degrees. Turn slices over; continue baking for 5 to 7 minutes. Let cool and drizzle with white chocolate, if desired; store in an airtight container. Makes about 3 dozen cookies.

Jo Ann
Gooseberry Patch

yummy iced mochas

Make your own iced mocha beverage...so refreshing, and there's no need for a trip to the coffee shop! Mix one cup brewed, chilled coffee with ½ cup milk and sugar to taste. Then add a teaspoon or two of chocolate syrup. Pour over crushed ice in a tall glass, relax, and enjoy!

White Chocolate Macaroons

Ready-made cookie dough makes these super simple.

18-oz. tube refrigerated white
    chocolate chunk cookie
    dough, at room temperature

2¼ c. sweetened flaked coconut
2 t. vanilla extract
½ t. coconut extract

Combine all ingredients; mix well. Drop by rounded teaspoonfuls onto ungreased baking sheets; bake at 350 degrees for 10 to 12 minutes. Cool on baking sheets for 2 minutes; remove to wire rack to cool completely. Makes 2 dozen cookies.

Dottie McCraw
Oklahoma City, OK

white chocolate drizzle

Give pastries a special touch with a drizzle of white chocolate! Briefly microwave a small plastic zipping bag filled with white chocolate chips until chips are melted. Snip off a tiny corner of the bag, and squeeze to drizzle; then toss the empty bag.

Peanut Butter-Chocolate Bars

Top with marshmallow creme for s'more fun!

1 c. creamy peanut butter
1 c. butter, melted
1 c. graham cracker crumbs

16-oz. pkg. powdered sugar
2 c. semi-sweet chocolate chips, melted

Combine first 4 ingredients together in a large mixing bowl; mix well using a wooden spoon. Press into the bottom of a well-greased 15"x10" jelly-roll pan; pour melted chocolate evenly over crust. Refrigerate for 15 minutes; score into bars but leave in pan. Refrigerate until firm; slice completely through scores, and serve cold. Makes 25 to 30 bars.

Eileen Blass
Catawissa, PA

Delicious Cookie Bars

Gooey and scrumptious treats!

A great recipe to introduce the kids to baking.

Kim

½ c. butter, melted
1½ c. graham cracker crumbs
14-oz. can sweetened condensed milk

12-oz. pkg. chocolate chips
1 c. peanut butter chips

In a lightly greased 13"x9" baking dish, pour in melted butter, and sprinkle with cracker crumbs. Pour milk evenly over crumbs; top with chocolate and peanut butter chips. Press down firmly. Bake, uncovered, at 350 degrees for 25 to 30 minutes. Makes 2 dozen bars.

Kim Olsen
Bridgeport, CT

Chocolate Chip Tea Cookies

(pictured on page 260)

These little cookies look so pretty yet are easy to make.

1 c. butter, softened
½ c. powdered sugar
1 t. vanilla extract

2 c. all-purpose flour
1½ c. mini semi-sweet chocolate
   chips, divided

With an electric mixer on high speed, beat butter and powdered sugar until fluffy. Add vanilla; mix well. Gradually beat in flour; use a spoon to stir in one cup chocolate chips. Form into one-inch balls; place 2 inches apart on ungreased baking sheets. Bake at 350 degrees for 10 to 12 minutes. Remove to wire rack to cool. Place remaining chocolate chips in a small plastic zipping bag. Seal bag; microwave on high until melted, about 30 seconds. Snip off a small corner of bag; drizzle chocolate over cooled cookies. Chill for 5 minutes, or until chocolate is set. Makes about 4 dozen cookies.

Michelle Sheridan
Upper Arlington, OH

When a friend asked me if I would bake cookies for a fundraiser, I didn't hesitate...I knew just what recipe to reach for!

Michelle

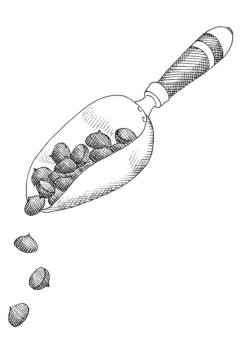

Grandma's Pecan Balls

Include this old-fashioned classic on your holiday sideboard.

1 c. butter, softened
⅓ c. sugar
2 t. vanilla extract

2 c. all-purpose flour
2 c. pecans, chopped
Garnish: powdered sugar

In a medium bowl, blend together butter and sugar; stir in vanilla and flour. Stir in pecans. Roll dough into walnut-size balls, and arrange on an ungreased baking sheet. Bake at 325 degrees for 45 minutes. While still warm, sprinkle cookies with powdered sugar; sprinkle again before serving. Makes about 2 dozen cookies.

Beckie Butcher
Elgin, IL

cookie jar magic

Keep your cookies moist! Place one slice of bread into a cookie jar or the storage bag, and your treats will stay soft.

Nichole's Cake Mix Cookies

These are a flavorful and moist, but not-too-sweet, cookie.

¼ c. butter, softened
8-oz. pkg. cream cheese, softened
1 egg yolk, beaten

½ t. vanilla extract
18¼-oz. pkg. butter pecan
  cake mix

With an electric mixer on medium speed, blend together butter and cream cheese. Add egg yolk and vanilla; blend thoroughly. Gradually beat in dry cake mix. Dough will be slightly stiff. Cover and refrigerate for 20 minutes. Drop dough by rounded teaspoonfuls onto greased or parchment paper-lined baking sheets. Bake at 350 degrees for 14 minutes or until lightly golden. Makes about 3 dozen.

Nichole Martelli
Santa Fe, TX

cookie cutter creations

Cookie cutter topiaries make sweet centerpieces for spring flings. Just secure a dowel in a terra cotta pot using sand or floral foam, glue a flower-shaped cookie cutter on top, and tie on a ribbon for the "leaves."

Snowballs

Covered in coconut flakes...there'll be no snowball fights with these!

1 c. semi-sweet chocolate chips
⅓ c. evaporated milk
1 c. powdered sugar

½ c. chopped walnuts
1¼ c. sweetened flaked coconut

Combine chocolate chips and milk in a double boiler; heat over hot water until chocolate melts. Stir to blend well. Remove from heat; stir in powdered sugar and nuts. Cool slightly. Form into one-inch balls; roll in coconut. Makes about 2 dozen.

Hope Davenport
Portland, TX

Here in South Texas we have to make these around the holidays, because they are the only snowballs we're going to see.

Hope

super shakers

Use a sugar shaker to save clean-up time in the kitchen. It's ideal for dusting powdered sugar onto cookies and desserts warm from the oven.

make-it-easy menus

holiday dinner

serves 6

*Slow-Cooker Creamy Apricot Chicken
(page 196)*

mashed potatoes

steamed asparagus

bakery rolls

Chocolate-Marshmallow Pie (page 269)

company coming

serves 6

Savory Cranberry Chicken (page 208)

stuffing

*Toasty Green Beans & Walnuts
(page 187)*

Grandmother's Pound Cake (page 275)

ladies' luncheon

serves 8

Egg Salad Minis (page 143)

Cranberry-Spinach Salad (page 122)

Minty Orange Iced Tea (page 39)

winter warm-up

serves 4 to 6

White Bean Chicken Chili (page 86)

Sour Cream Mini Biscuits (page 78)

weeknight supper

serves 6 to 8

Easy Chicken Dinner (page 232)

Cheesy Onion Muffins (page 80)

Italian night

serves 12

Quick & Easy Lasagna (page 202)

Parmesan-Garlic Biscuits (page 83)

tossed salad

Italian Zeppoli Bread (page 69)

fiesta feast

serves 12

Toss-It-Together Salsa (page 30)

Tamale Pie (page 218)

toppings and tortilla chips

tossed salad

bountiful brunch

serves 6

Festive Brunch Frittata (page 65)

fresh strawberries

Orange Slushy (page 39)

family night

serves 8

Family Favorite Chili Mac (page 207)

cornbread sticks

mixed salad greens

Delicious Cookie Bars (page 300)

game day get-together

serves 8 to 10

Reuben Bread-Bowl Dip (page 34)

Chinese Chicken Wings (page 243)
and celery sticks

Honey-Glazed Snack Mix (page 246)

Peanut Butter Bars (page 289)

open house

serves 8 to 10

Cheery Cherry Punch (page 45)

Holiday Stuffed Mushrooms (page 27)

Feta Cheese Ball (page 10)

Easiest-Ever Cheesecake (page 265)

breakfast for dinner

serves 8

Beef & Cheddar Quiche (page 53)

salsa and sour cream

Anytime Cheesy Biscuits (page 75)

backyard picnic

serves 4

Weekend Treat Burgers (page 140)

Spicy Carrot French Fries (page 161)

Open-Face Peach Pie (page 266)

summer garden celebration

serves 4

Toasted Green Tomato Sandwiches (page 136)

Quick & Easy Veggie Salad (page 118)

Berry Crumble (page 271)

just for kids

serves 4 to 6

Marshmallow Fruit Dip (page 238)

Pepperoni Pizza Bites (page 240)

*Caramel-Marshmallow Delights
(page 258)*

cookie-exchange party

serves 4 to 6

Chocolate Chip Tea Cookies (page 301)

Snowballs (page 307)

White Chocolate Macaroons (page 298)

Nichole's Cake Mix Cookies (page 304)

hot chocolate

METRIC EQUIVALENTS

The recipes that appear in this cookbook use the standard U.S. method for measuring liquid and dry or solid ingredients (teaspoons, tablespoons, and cups). The information in the following charts is provided to help cooks outside the United States successfully use these recipes. All equivalents are approximate.

METRIC EQUIVALENTS FOR DIFFERENT TYPES OF INGREDIENTS

A standard cup measure of a dry or solid ingredient will vary in weight depending on the type of ingredient.
A standard cup of liquid is the same volume for any type of liquid. Use the following chart when converting standard cup measures to grams (weight) or milliliters (volume).

Standard Cup	Fine Powder (ex. flour)	Grain (ex. rice)	Granular (ex. sugar)	Liquid Solids (ex. butter)	Liquid (ex. milk)
1	140 g	150 g	190 g	200 g	240 ml
¾	105 g	113 g	143 g	150 g	180 ml
⅔	93 g	100 g	125 g	133 g	160 ml
½	70 g	75 g	95 g	100 g	120 ml
⅓	47 g	50 g	63 g	67 g	80 ml
¼	35 g	38 g	48 g	50 g	60 ml
⅛	18 g	19 g	24 g	25 g	30 ml

USEFUL EQUIVALENTS FOR LIQUID INGREDIENTS BY VOLUME

¼ tsp	=					1 ml
½ tsp	=					2 ml
1 tsp	=					5 ml
3 tsp	= 1 tbls		= ½ fl oz	=	15 ml
	2 tbls	= ⅛ cup	= 1 fl oz	=	30 ml
	4 tbls	= ¼ cup	= 2 fl oz	=	60 ml
	5⅓ tbls	= ⅓ cup	= 3 fl oz	=	80 ml
	8 tbls	= ½ cup	= 4 fl oz	=	120 ml
	10⅔ tbls	= ⅔ cup	= 5 fl oz	=	160 ml
	12 tbls	= ¾ cup	= 6 fl oz	=	180 ml
	16 tbls	= 1 cup	= 8 fl oz	=	240 ml
1 pt	= 2 cups	= 16 fl oz	=	480 ml
1 qt	= 4 cups	= 32 fl oz	=	960 ml
			33 fl oz	= 1000 ml = 1 liter

USEFUL EQUIVALENTS FOR DRY INGREDIENTS BY WEIGHT

(To convert ounces to grams, multiply the number of ounces by 30.)

1 oz	=	¹⁄₁₆ lb	=	30 g
4 oz	=	¼ lb	=	120 g
8 oz	=	½ lb	=	240 g
12 oz	=	¾ lb	=	360 g
16 oz	=	1 lb	=	480 g

USEFUL EQUIVALENTS FOR LENGTH

(To convert inches to centimeters, multiply the number of inches by 2.5.)

1 in =		= 2.5 cm	
6 in =	½ ft	= 15 cm	
12 in =	1 ft	= 30 cm	
36 in =	3 ft = 1 yd	= 90 cm	
40 in =		= 100 cm	= 1 meter

USEFUL EQUIVALENTS FOR COOKING/OVEN TEMPERATURES

	Fahrenheit	Celsius	Gas Mark
Freeze Water	32° F	0° C	
Room Temperature	68° F	20° C	
Boil Water	212° F	100° C	
Bake	325° F	160° C	3
	350° F	180° C	4
	375° F	190° C	5
	400° F	200° C	6
	425° F	220° C	7
	450° F	230° C	8
Broil			Grill

index

My Favorite Recipes

Our Story

Back in 1984, we were next-door neighbors raising our families in the little town of Delaware, Ohio. Two moms with small children, we were looking for a way to do what we loved and stay home with the kids too. We had always shared a love of home cooking and making memories with family & friends and so, after many a conversation over the backyard fence, **Gooseberry Patch** was born.

We put together our first catalog at our kitchen tables, enlisting the help of our loved ones wherever we could. From that very first mailing, we found an immediate connection with many of our customers and it wasn't long before we began receiving letters, photos and recipes from these new friends. In 1992, we put together our very first cookbook, compiled from hundreds of these recipes and, the rest, as they say, is history.

Hard to believe it's been over 25 years since those kitchen-table days! From that original little Gooseberry Patch family, we've grown to include an amazing group of creative folks who love cooking, decorating and creating as much as we do. Today, we're best known for our homestyle, family-friendly cookbooks, now recognized as national bestsellers.

One thing's for sure, we couldn't have done it without our friends all across the country. Each year, we're honored to turn thousands of your recipes into our collectible cookbooks. Our hope is that each book captures the stories and heart of all of you who have shared with us. Whether you've been with us since the beginning or are just discovering us, welcome to the **Gooseberry Patch** family!

Your friends at Gooseberry Patch

We couldn't make our best-selling cookbooks without YOU!

Each of our books is filled with recipes from cooks just like you, gathered from kitchens all across the country.

Share your tried & true recipes with us on our website and you could be selected for an upcoming cookbook. If your recipe is included, you'll receive a FREE copy of the cookbook when it's published!

www.gooseberrypatch.com

We'd love to add YOU to our Circle of Friends!

Get free recipes, crafts, giveaways and so much more when you join our email club...join us online at all the spots below for even more goodies!

Join our Circle of Friends

Subscribe on **You Tube**

f Find us on Facebook

Read Our **Blog**

Follow us on **twitter**

Follow us on **Pinterest**